GO AHEAD AND ASK!

INTERVIEWS ABOUT SCREENWRITING (AND PIE)

VOLUME TWO

MORE BAKING, MORE MOVIES!

PAUL E. ZEIDMAN

GO AHEAD & ASK

INTERVIEWS ABOUT SCREENWRITING (AND PIE)

VOLUME TWO

Cover design and Interior Formatting: Cali Gilbert

Published in the United States of America

First Printing, July, 2022

To learn more about author, Paul E. Zeidman, visit
http://maximumz.blog

Endorsements

Andrew Hilton/The Screenplay Mechanic

Paul has amassed a huge and diverse network of writers and industry professionals and that has enabled him to truly tap into the pulse of the screenwriting world. Using that wealth of knowledge, he's gained some remarkable insights and can now share that wisdom with you as you begin your own screenwriting odyssey. He's also the nation's foremost expert on all things pie.

Ryan Dixon/Tartan Valley Ventures

Paul Zeidman is an ideal guide into the art, craft and business of screenwriting. The interviews in this collection offer tips, tools and strategies that are invaluable and essential for anyone pursuing a screenwriting career.

J.G. Sarantinos/Creative Screenwriting

The best scripts are the ones when writers tap into raw emotions. When writers are told to write what they know, it should be, write the emotions you know. That will ground your story no matter how you execute it.

Jeff Kitchen/Scriptwriting Mastery

Paul is a dynamic interviewer who asks highly specific questions that get to the heart of the matter and evoke deep responses. Plus he's a serious writer himself so that he brings a wealth of knowledge and experience to the process. And he's a pleasure to work with.

Howard Casner/Rantings & Ravings

I recommend everyone who is an aspiring writer, and maybe even those further ahead, to check out these interviews. They can be a valuable resource to forging a career in the industry. These are more practical and immediately applicable pieces of advice on getting ahead, not just articles on how to write a good and/or marketable screenplay. I enjoyed very much doing the interview, but in reading it again, perhaps one thing has changed: today, more and more, the first two or three projects, a screenwriter will probably have to find a way to do those themselves, whether shorts, web series or features. That's just the way the industry is today. Another change: I still love pie, but now have diabetes, so that part of my life for the most part is over. Ah, well.

Jim Cirile/Coverage Ink

Paul Zeidman has achieved a rather remarkable feat: he's compressed years of practical screenwriting knowledge into a very small space. Via a series of interviews wherein he asks the same questions of a panoply of industry experts, a compelling and indisputable how-to-do-it quickly emerges. A powerful blast of useful intelligence that writers at any level should benefit from.

Phil Clarke/Philmscribe Script Consultancy

Being quizzed by Paul the pie guy was a pleasurable experience. He knows just what to ask in order to get to the nitty gritty, his focused questions helping to deliver answers that I have no doubt will provide real nuggets of gold for aspiring screenwriters out there - not to mention pie lovers!

Staton Rabin/Screenwriter and Script Analyst (ScreenplayMuse.com)

If there were an Oscar for "Most Generous Screenwriter", Paul Zeidman deserves to get it. He's always sharing valuable information, and offering his time and positive energy to help aspiring screenwriters. Paul is an award-winning screenwriter who has been in the trenches himself, so when he interviewed me for his blog, Maximum Z, I knew he'd ask exactly the kinds of questions that would really help writers who are trying to break in. And he did!

Table of Contents

Note from the Author

After completing my first set of interviews with screenwriting consultants for my blog Maximum Z (http://maximumz.blog), I'd discovered that there were still more out there, all eager and willing to share their thoughts and opinions.

I'd also started connecting with writers in other mediums, who also had helpful advice on writing in general. Even though they don't write scripts, a lot of what they have to say still applies to overall storytelling.

The result - this book.

Some of the consultants and writers included in this volume have also written books targeted specifically at screenwriters. I make it a point to read their book before interviewing them, so I can vouch for the solid advice in each one. Any would make a great addition to your personal library (as well make for a great resource while working on your latest script).

And like with the previous volume, feel free to indulge yourself with a slice of your favorite pie (possibly the same kind as one of the names here) as you peruse the sage advice offered within these pages.

Thanks for reading!

Paul

Babz Bitela

Originally posted: Aug 19 2016

Barbara "Babz" Bitela is a literary manager operating out of northern California, a "hired gun" editor for fiction writers, and hosts the Babzbuzz internet radio show "because folks were nice to me and helped me, so I'm trying to pay it forward, and believe me, I'm keeping it real."

"We want voice on the page. We KNOW it when we 'hear' it."

Her book STORY OF A ROCK SINGER is currently being adapted as a Broadway musical.

What's the last thing you watched/read that you thought was incredibly well-written?

JUSTIFIED and BATES MOTEL are my top two. Joss Whedon is by far one of my favorite writers. BUFFY the TV series – WOW! You can youtube his interviews: it's like an AA degree in writing and it's free to anyone.

How'd you get your start doing representation?

I pitched a semi-retired agent named Ed Silver on a book I wrote. He was Lee Marvin's manager and finance guy, also for James Coburn and many others. The guy's 'seen' stuff, man – Hitchcock napping, for one. He loved my style and offered me a gig to take over and he'd mentor. We clicked big time. He's Jewish, I'm

Italian. As Sebastian Maniscalco says, "Same corporation, different division." That's us.

Is recognizing good writing something you believe can be taught or learned?

You for sure can learn it IF you want to. Here's why – bad writing obviously sucks. It just does. How do you know that? By reading GREAT (not just good) scripts. I read so much so often I can now tell what's going to go and what MAY go but here's the rub: in the absence of money behind it, it may not matter. And I may love it and another may say "meh". So POV does matter.

So you can learn and pitch but Lady Luck is no lady: she's a tramp in cheap shoes and she's fickle. We press on because we believe in the story/writer we hawk. If it goes, it goes, if it doesn't, well, I've had the benefit of "seeing" incredible "movies" and the only down side is, so few others will see that. THE WRITER however, benefits. Why? Job well done. And if you don't write for the JOY of the craft, there's no point. Write for the sale? That's an industry sucker punch. I've learned to find great scripts and I've learned it can be like screaming in space once you do.

What are the components of a good script?

VOICE, RISING ACTION and TWISTS. What is voice: it's a lot like porn – I know it when I see it but it's hard to describe. Think of it this way: you open a novel, settle in and by page two you're thinking "Ugh, this just sucks", but you press on and by page ten you know it's not the book for you so you donate it to Goodwill.

It's the same with a script. I once read a TV pilot by my client that I couldn't read it fast enough. Why? I WAS DYING TO SEE WHERE IT WOULD LEAD. The action and characters were alive on the page. That is what makes a good script: I call it NARRATIVE TUG.

What are some of the most common mistakes you see?

Where to start? Typos, for sure. It's a speed bump.

- Wrylies. Just don't. UGH! Makes me crazy. There's only one time I've seen it used where it worked. ONCE. And that writer is a five-figure-income writer.
- Novels posing as scripts. The writer MUST understand the economy of words and do VISUAL storytelling. Telling a story with pictures is a movie. Telling a story with talking is a soap opera.
- Avoid using "ing" words – slows narrative, slows the readers eyes.
- Avoid "very". Just find what IT IS. Don't say "very smart", say "bright" – just pick! Not kidding. You'll thank me. J.I. Rodale's THE SYNONYM FINDER is invaluable for writers.

And never fall in love with your stuff. It's gonna get cut.

What story tropes are you tired of seeing?

Well, many work. Some don't. My favorite recently was probably in draft form: "Fire all phasers!" But instead he said "Fire everything!" Love it!

But I say write bad and cliché in the draft, leave it there, then go back and rewrite it.

Lots of folks say "Not my first rodeo." I say "Not my first rocket launch." Anything to WAKE UP the reader.

What are the three most important rules every writer should know?

I've got more than three.

- Don't enter a script contest pitching a word doc.
- Don't send a script unless invited.
- Don't ask me what I think if you don't want to know.
- Don't go past 120 pages. I mean it. Try to stay around 100 if you can.

More rules? I think it's just wise to do 12pt Courier font as it's tradition. The Coen Brothers don't use Courier. But they're already famous, so when you're famous do what you want. In the meantime, stick to tradition.

What do you look for when it comes to potential clients, both personally and professionally?
No dope. No booze. No drama.

Feet on the ground, and committed to spending tons of time doing what you love, regardless of the outcome.

My clients pitch themselves. They must. If that's not for you, then I'm not the manager for you, and also, you're in the wrong business.

Yes, the manager makes inroads, but you must pitch you and build relationships. When you do; AVOID using "I" and ask the person "What do you do, and how do you do it?" Ask about them. We're people FIRST. That's why I do Babzbuzz. People like me. They helped me. So I take what they tell me and mush it up with what I've learned, and talk about it on my show to try to help.

I'm a small company: I'm WGA.

Meh. Folks hang up on me all the time.

Why?

"Babz, love the script! Who's funding?"

Crickets.

"Babz, baby. Call us back when you have the dough and I'll show my client. He may want to star in it."

EEEK!

What happened to love of story?

Hell, that left the building and moved to an island the actor/director owns. He's got to feed his family too, ya know. So bring the bricks.

EEEK!

Lightning can and does strike. That's what I do. I'm really a stormchaser who looks for folks with money who want to buy.

Readers of this blog are more than familiar with my love and appreciation of pie. What's your favorite kind?

Oh man, you had me at the fridge door. Dutch apple. Key lime. Rhubarb when you can find it. And pretty much any clever use of chocolate.

Jeff Buitenveld/ScriptArsenal

Originally posted: Apr 12 2019

Jeff Buitenveld of ScriptArsenal is an independent producer and former development executive with over 15 years of experience on some of Hollywood's biggest films. He is currently a producer on the upcoming thriller THE KIMBERLITE PROCESS. After graduating with an MFA from UCLA's Producers Program, Jeff worked in various capacities on numerous productions for Tom Cruise and Paula Wagner including THE LAST SAMURAI, MISSION IMPOSSIBLE 3, JACK REACHER, VALKYRIE, LIONS FOR LAMBS starring Robert Redford and Meryl Streep, ASK THE DUST starring Colin Farrell and Salma Hayek, DEATH RACE starring Jason Statham, THE EYE starring Jessica Alba, SUSPECT ZERO starring Aaron Eckhart and Ben Kingsley and many more.

What's the last thing you read or watched that you thought was incredibly well-written?

SPIDER-MAN: INTO THE SPIDER-VERSE was a blast. HBO's BARRY is a funny and oddly haunting series. I recently re-watched/re-read HELL OR HIGH WATER, which is a deceptively simple, sad, and suspenseful story with rich, complicated characters. Netflix's THE HAUNTING OF HILL HOUSE delivered the goods on scares and family dysfunction for me. Issa Rae (INSECURE), Jill Soloway (TRANSPARENT), Amy Sherman-Palladino (THE MARVELOUS MRS. MAISEL), and Andrea Savage (I'M SORRY) all have unique, exciting, and powerful voices.

How'd you get your start in the industry?

I didn't know anyone in LA when I first moved here but developed a sci-fi project that was quickly optioned by an Academy Award-winning producer (and never made). During that time, I was also accepted into UCLA's Producers Program where I took Meg Le Fauve's (INSIDE OUT, CAPTAIN MARVEL) Development class, which was instrumental to my growth and understanding of cinematic storytelling and how to work effectively with screenwriters.

I started cold-calling various companies for internships and was lucky enough to land positions at both Artisan Entertainment and Mike Medavoy's Phoenix Pictures. Back then, Artisan had a deal with Marvel and I was immediately thrown into pitch meetings with various notable writers/directors on properties like Thor, Hulk, The Punisher, Black Widow, and Iron Fist, etc. I was also taking pitches at Phoenix – it was an incredible learning experience. I eventually became an assistant briefly to a Hong Kong action director and then used those experiences to land a job with Tom Cruise and Paula Wagner once I graduated from UCLA.

Is recognizing good writing something you think can be taught or learned?

Though having an eye for quality material can be a natural instinct, it needs to be honed. I ultimately feel that recognizing good writing can be learned and taught.

What do you consider the components of a good script?

Generally speaking, a good script maintains a captivating concept, and a flawed but likeable hero with a concrete objective attached to grave stakes (whether intimate or epic). The hero's emotional flaw is often rectified as a result of him/her achieving their practical goal (he/she should also be active, resourceful, and exhibit a range of change). It's helpful if the hero's goal is time-sensitive and somehow socially relevant. Lastly, if the script is a feature, it should adhere to a three-act structure.

What are some of the most common screenwriting mistakes you see?

Too much description, on-the-nose dialogue, flimsy structure, and the lack of a flawed hero with a concrete objective, attached to grave stakes.

What story tropes are you just tired of seeing?

I'm not at all opposed to writers using things like "one last job," "a reluctant hero who can save the world," "a family in peril," or "a fish out of water," etc. The familiar can be very accessible and., if used effectively, can lure a reader into the story. The trick, however, is to infuse that story with other unique and complex qualities so that it unfolds in fresh and unexpected ways. What can make your story different or set it apart? I always urge writers to challenge the reader's expectations or preconceived notions as to what type of story they're entering!

What are some key rules/guidelines every writer should know?

- Use Final Draft.
- Study the most notable screenwriting books and authors.
- Read every script you can get your hands on whether good, bad, or mediocre.
- Have conviction but be open to ideas – ultimately this is a collaborative industry.
- Don't be afraid of genre and don't be afraid to push the boundaries on the tenets of said genre (but know what those tenets are).
- Actively seek feedback and don't be precious.
- Strive to be both clear and complex in your writing and understand the difference between the two.
- Don't be a hater – watch all kinds of movies and TV shows, and be mindful of those that are both commercially and critically successful as well as those that aren't.
- Read the trades to better understand the marketplace.
- Don't chase trends – write from the heart.

Have you ever read a spec script that was an absolute, without-a-doubt "recommend"? If so, what were the reasons why?

"Recommends" are a rare breed. Those that do qualify show a master of the craft, are usually somewhat familiar but also somehow unique, tend to maintain complex characters, rich themes, and have an easily identifiable position in the marketplace (you can visualize the poster, trailer, audience, etc.) That being said, most of the scripts I've read, even from the most notable A-list writers in the industry, still needed some further development.

How do you feel about screenwriting contests? Worth it or not?

I think it can be incredibly important and worthwhile, particularly for young writers, to enter screenwriting contests. However, I would also encourage writers to do some homework on which ones are notable and relevant so as to not waste too much money and time.

How can people find out more about you and the services you provide?

Go to www.scriptarsenal.com and follow us on FaceBook and Twitter (@scriptarsenal) to get updates on upcoming sales and weekly helpful screenwriting tips.

Readers of this blog are more than familiar with my love/appreciation of pie. What's your favorite kind?

Given my mid-section I generally try to stay away from sweets, but a few years ago, I had some homemade pecan pie (numerous pieces actually) for Thanksgiving and it was an absolutely transformative experience...a chemical portal to another dimension that somehow transcended the time-space continuum...okay, maybe I'm being a bit dramatic but damn, it was good!

Geoffrey D. Calhoun/We Fix Your Script

Originally posted: Oct 20 2017

Geoffrey D. Calhoun of wefixyourscript.com is listed as a Top 100 Indie Writer in the World. He has optioned several screenplays and has worked as a writer on two features coming out in 2017: THE LITTLE GIRL and STUDIO 5. His multi-award-winning thriller PINK BUNNY is scheduled for a 2018 release. Geoffrey has won multiple screenwriting awards and has worked as a producer, an assistant director, and director on indie film productions. He has been sought out by studios as a script consultant and a re-writer for various stages of development and production.

What's the last thing you read/watched that you thought was incredibly well-written?

The last thing I watched I couldn't stop thinking about was ARRIVAL. I loved this film. It had depth and really explored her character. I loved how they played around with the structure of the film in creative ways that really built up to a climax. It was fantastic. I could see how Eric Heisserer did over 100 drafts to make that story perfect.

How'd you get your start reading scripts?

I actually began writing on a bet. A friend of mine was an editor for a local kids show. He wanted to push himself to write a script so he challenged me to see who could write better. Personally, I wasn't interested because I have dyslexia. I agreed to do it, and ended up really enjoying the process. Since then it became more than a passion, almost like a volition. I wanted to be the best screenwriter I could possibly be, so I started studying and learning from the greats such as Syd Field, Robert McKee, Viki King and reading screenplays by modern legends as well like David Goyer, Jonathan Nolan, and Christopher McQuarrie.

Is recognizing good writing something you think can be taught or learned?

I think it can be learned. It comes with time. The average movie attendee can recognize a bad film. Now, some people prefer bad films, but that's a whole different form of self- torture (wink). I like this question. It reminds me of the debate about raw talent vs. learned skill. Some teachers out there believe if you don't have a modicum of innate talent with writing, then you'll never be a good writer. I completely disagree with this. Their defense is that this is an art, and thus you must have a certain amount of "taste" in order to know the difference between what's good and bad.

I think what we do is more than an art. It's a craft; a learned skill plain and simple. Something that can be mastered with just two things, time and practice. That's all you need. We are craftsmen, like the blacksmiths of old. At first creating something small and simple like a horseshoe, then with time we master our skill and create compelling stories and works of art like the ornate armors of old.

What are the components of a good script?

It all starts with having something to say in your script. What are we trying to pass off to the audience? What do we want to tell them about life? Something that will open their eyes and help them see things from a new perspective? Or something that will reassure them and speak to the struggles they are going through? When we have a theme like this and we pair it with a sympathetic character, then we create a compelling story that's unforgettable and emotionally moving. Take ARRIVAL. It's about a woman's struggle with loss. That's something that speaks to everyone, which is why it resonated so well with people.

What are some of the most common mistakes you see?

Wow, that's a tough one. I see mistakes of all kinds from new screenwriters to professionals. One mistake I often see is having underdeveloped characters. They're superficial and are around just to be a face. Sometimes they're even described as pretty or handsome, which reinforces this.

When I get hired for a rewrite, the first thing I do is take the characters and layer in depth to make them more human and sympathetic; give them reasons to do what they're doing and why they make the choices they do. I create depth by adding to them traits that we all suffer from but never talk about such as secretly insecure, lonely, or lost, etc.

What story tropes are you just tired of seeing?

This is more a genre thing for me but I'm sick of the false ending in horror films. Here we spend at least 90 minutes emotionally involved with a character. If it's a good one – Dawn of the Dead is a good example – then you'll have me on my seat the entire film. Then at the end, the lucky few characters that have survived finally make it…until there's a surprise jump scare right before the credits roll and we discover the characters we'd been rooting for this whole time never make it. I'm so frustrated by this. For me it feels like a waste of my time to discover they all die because of a dirty trope in the end.

What are the 3 most important rules every writer should know?

STEAL: Steal everything from everyone. Writers are the best thieves in the world. I'm not saying plagiarize, but when you find a technique or scene that really works for you, break it down and make it your own so you can add it to your toolbox.

STUDY: This goes with stealing. Learn from the masters. Writers like John August have a blog that you should be following. Don't stop there. Learn from the masters that taught the master such as Aristotle. If you pay attention, all the great screenwriters will quote Aristotle. There's a reason for that.

IGNORE THE BS: There's a lot of flack out there towards aspiring screenwriters. I recently read an article where a Hollywood writer was bragging about telling screenwriters they'll never make it. He tells them they should just give up because they aren't talented. It's BS. You can make it, but it takes time. A long time. If a dyslexic from Detroit can make it, then you can too. One of the reasons I founded wefixyourscript.com was exactly for that purpose: to give screenwriters that extra helping hand to not just improve upon their screenplays, but to help them become better screenwriters. That's why we include a one-on-one consultation.

Have you ever read a script that was an absolute, without-a-doubt "recommend"? If so, could you give the logline?

Definitely. In fact, I just did some coverage on a dramatic short that had a fantastic concept. I helped them tweak it, but only a little. I guarantee it won't have a dry eye in the audience when it films. Unfortunately, that's all I can say about it.

How do you feel about screenwriting contests? Worth it or not?

I think they're great, and I strongly recommend contests in festivals. That's where you can really make headway as a writer. You need to network and make connections to build up your reputation. You can meet other writers, producers, and directors that will eventually land you in a spot where you'll be getting work. When you go to these fests you want to be the life of the party. Have fun. Get yourself out there. And make sure you're handing out business cards. It will get you work.

How can people can get in touch with you to find out more about the services you provide?

They can contact us at info@wefixyourscript.com. They can also sign up for a free 15-minute consultation on our website. With our consultation, we offer ways to help your work or answer any questions about us or the industry in general. We've had some great feedback on this service.

Readers of this blog are more than familiar with my love/appreciation of pie. What's your favorite kind?

I've got to go with mom's pumpkin pie. There is one caveat though: it must be smothered with a big dollop of whipped cream.

Emma T. Capps

Originally posted: Oct 27 2017

Being a lifelong reader of comic books, it was inevitable I would discover and subsequently enjoy a wide variety of webcomics. Variety is actually one of the key words in play here. There are so many to choose from, along with so much talent on display from the creators.

Like with screenplays, webcomics are great examples of storytelling – just in a different medium. It takes a lot of work to create and maintain a quality webcomic.

I first met Emma Capps at the Alternative Press Expo in San Francisco; she was 15 years old and already an accomplished cartoonist. She's experienced a lot since then, both professionally and personally, and despite some tough setbacks, still maintains an incredibly positive and upbeat attitude.

"Emma T. Capps started her first webcomic at age 14, and has exhibited her work all over the country and done special installments for publications like Dark Horse Presents. She also teaches cartooning workshops at 826 Valencia in San Francisco, and has more than doubled the percentage of female students in her classes! In her spare time, she likes chatting in Spanish, learning new crafts, and being politically active through volunteer work. Most of all, she really hates talking about herself in the third person."

What's the last thing you read/watched that you thought was incredibly well-written?

Hmm, this is honestly a bit of a tough one to answer because I am constantly reading. I just finished George Saunders' LINCOLN IN THE BARDO, which to my mind deserves all the accolades it's recently gotten. (Michiko Kakutani, recently departed bastion of the New York Times book review, never steers me astray). BARDO is a bit of a tricky book to classify, as it skillfully combines various genres in a way that makes it difficult to define. I cried much more than I expected for a book where the premise is that all the characters are dead.

I think what I recently had the most fun reading was Scott Hawkins' THE LIBRARY AT MOUNT CHAR, a novel that to me has flown quite undeservedly under the radar. It's a really fresh voice in fantasy that begs multiple readings just because it is so skillfully plotted and imagined. There are scenes of violence and horror – many – but I've still been recommending it all around and it's become one of my favorite books. It begs a sequel, or a companion novel set within the same universe, but as of yet Hawkins hasn't expressed his immediate plans to write one (LIBRARY is remarkably, his debut).

In terms of things I've watched, I don't watch a large amount of TV – mostly period dramas, like DOWNTON ABBEY, CALL THE MIDWIFE and pretty much everything on Masterpiece Classic – but a movie that has one of the most excellent scripts, to me, is Tarsem's THE FALL. This might be a little bit of a cop-out because there were definitely unscripted scenes between the young actress and Lee Pace, but the entire conceit of the movie is amazing – and the costumes by Eiko Ishioka are understandably incredible. It's a historical movie, sure, but at its core it's a movie about the power of stories and how they bind us all together.

How'd you get into creating your own comics?

This is also unfortunately a slightly strange answer. It's not so cut-and-dry! I always knew I loved writing and drawing, and I had several short stories I published in STONE SOUP MAGAZINE along with illustrations I did. But I never really synthesized the two, mostly because I considered my writing to be better developed than my art skills were at that point. But I took a short art course, and I realized I actually could capture my ideas visually just as I had imagined them.

In Fall 2010, I drew a short autobiographical comic called JAM DAYS and submitted it to a competition – and, somehow, managed to work that into my final "recital" project for 8th grade. But I finished JAM far before the overall project's deadline! So, I re-discovered Chapel, a character I had created a while ago and had turned into a line of greeting cards I made for my parents. I've always had a fascination with newspaper dailies, which are sadly dying out, and I thought it would be a great challenge to try and recreate that sort of schedule.

So I set out to draw one Chapel comic every single day for 30 days. I put them online in installments – that's what became "Season One" of THE CHAPEL CHRONICLES – and by the time I'd finished posting them, I realized they had really struck a chord. People were commenting! People I didn't even know in real life! So why not continue? I lightened my load a little bit, though, to one comic per week instead of per day. I kept to that schedule throughout all four years of high school (including summer break!)

What are some of your favorite comics and webcomics?

My favorite comics hew much more to the print side than the webcomic side, although some of them were definitely webcomics that later become print collections! My favorite print volumes are Mazzucchelli's ASTERIOS POLYP, Kerascoet's BEAUTIFUL DARKNESS, DeForge's ANT COLONY, Tamaki's SUPERMUTANT MAGIC ACADEMY (previously serialized online, but I strongly recommend the printed version).

In terms of series, I really enjoy Oda's ONE PIECE – I use it as an example of differing panel structures in the comics classes I teach. In a parallel universe where I actually have my life together, I'd also keep up regularly with WITCHY, PARANATURAL, SAINT FOR RENT, and HARK! A VAGRANT. I'm 99.99999% sure there are more that I'm forgetting to list.

In our pre-interview, you'd mentioned plotting out the story for your latest project. How did you come up with the idea for it, and how did you develop it?

In contrast to Chapel, this story, THE LEAGUE OF FONTS, is much older in terms of its sheer gestation period. I actually had the idea for it before I even started doing Chapel! If I remember correctly, I was having lunch with my grandma and had the idea – but I had no paper, so I went to a stationary store next door and bought a small notebook to jot down my thoughts! I still have the notebook, somewhere.

The structure of the story was far different back then, but the central conceit of the characters and fonts was the same. It has evolved through various iterations and plot changes, though, especially as I learned things that could make certain aspects more realistic and others less so for the purpose of satire. I think my greatest breakthrough was a few years ago, when I realized it was a highly visual story and would be better served as a graphic novel instead of a prose story. So I converted it to a script, and continued work in that format. I have the entire story scripted now, on Scrivener, which for me is the ideal process: that way, when I'm actually drawing, I can put all my attention on the visual aspect knowing that I've already got the overall flow of the storyline planned out. If I hadn't done that writing beforehand, it would be a mess, since it's a highly detailed plot and relies on continuity to really work.

Going through the archives of THE CHAPEL CHRONICLES, some of the earlier strips are of the one-and-done format, followed by a gradual transition into longer storylines. Was this intentional or more of a natural progression (i.e. the more you wrote, the more ideas you got)?

As I mentioned previously, I didn't really have a set "game plan" for how I would start Chapel – and, honestly, I never intended it to become something longer. My first 30-comics-in-30-days was a personal challenge, but I found I enjoyed it much more than I had anticipated. There's still narrative and continuity in those early comics; some of the board game strips, for example, might not make quite as much sense without context, nor would the storyline of Chapel acquiring her pet hedgehog, Rupert. Once I decided I was going to make more Chapel, I immediately knew there would be longer storylines. My favorite newspaper comics do just that: there are longer storylines, but each can still be enjoyable as a stand-alone strip.

You're definitely a very creative person. Is being a professional artist/cartoonist the ultimate goal, or just one of many?

I honestly don't know! YES, being a professional cartoonist is a life dream of mine – but is it the only, ultimate goal? Most likely not.

When it comes to stand-alone visual art, I doubt it. This goes against all accepted artist etiquette, but I almost never sketch. If I do, it's to plan out aspects of a narrative world I'm creating. I don't mind that, though! I have little-to-no interest in being solely a visual artist, as I honestly don't think that's my strong suit.

When I was younger I wanted to be a novelist, and I still might revisit that – comics, to me, are just a way of telling stories that have a strong visual component and couldn't be fully expressed with just prose. I read books all the time (to the point where I've had to ban myself from reading the New York Times book review, since it's the equivalent of window-shopping for me) and I feel, often, the narrative/written side of graphic novels is treated as less important than the strength of the artwork. Really, the opposite is true. The most successful contemporary comics don't, in a strict sense, have technical artistic proficiency. The reason they're so popular is because the story or writing has something that is engaging. XKCD, for example, pulls no punches: it's all stick figures, but it's so wildly popular because it resonates with people through the strength of the writing.

When I was a lot younger, I wanted to be a paleontologist, but now I'm not sure I'd be a very good one. Math and science aren't really my strong suits – they could be, if I was passionate about them enough to study them on my own – so that likely wouldn't work out. In my spare time, beyond reading, I like to design and sew/knit my own clothes. But as of yet, I have no intention of ever doing that professionally. That way, nobody can see my lazy seam-work on the interior of the garment! I mostly taught myself, so I don't do anything the way it's "supposed" to be done. If it fits, then I'm happy, and I don't have to go clothes shopping ever again!

You've taught cartooning workshops at a non-profit writing center. How did that come about, and what sort of things do you talk about?

Coinciding with my initial work on THE CHAPEL CHRONICLES, I decided I would bundle up the first "season" into a small book and sell it at my school's craft/project fair! I also went to a convention (my first one ever!) in New York and exhibited there as well, which was terrifying, exhausting, and exhilarating all at once. I had planned from the beginning to donate all my profits to 826 Valencia, a nonprofit in San Francisco, as one of the teachers who first sparked my interest in creating comics used to teach there. They were a bit surprised at a 14-year-old donating money, I think, and invited me to come teach a comic class myself! I was unimaginably nervous, but I wanted to knock it out of the park, so I prepared worksheets on the process, a detailed time breakdown for the class, and specific PowerPoint presentations on what I'd be trying to teach. I really wanted to show them that I wasn't doing this just as a lark (or, in any way, a "volunteer experience" to look good on school applications). I was serious!

My first workshop was a disaster: only one student showed up. 826 contacted me to apologize, and asked if I'd like to teach another class. I didn't, but I said yes regardless. I started to teach regularly, and began theming my workshops so students could have some framework around which to create their ideas. Mostly, I focused on teaching kids various steps of planning a comic, and then some conventional tools that make cartooning easier – but my focus was never about imposing some specific way of doing something, as I'd experienced that in art classes at my school and bristled at it. I would explain to them why we would be doing a certain step, and why I felt it was helpful. I'd then go around to each student individually, and if they had a reason they'd like to do something against the grain, I would encourage them to go for it! I really wanted to let their individual voices shine. I even had a few "repeat offenders" who attended multiple classes and tried to squeak in before registration filled up, as it did often!

I love teaching, and I haven't gotten to do so in a while due to extenuating circumstances, which leads me to...

You also mentioned having to take a break from writing and drawing due to some health issues. Can you elaborate on that, and how are you feeling these days?

I would be more than happy to discuss it! To be honest, I'm never quite sure how to bring up the details – I've essentially disappeared for the greater part of two years, both to focus on my treatment and to figure out a way to broach the subject. I'm always cognizant that the Chapel audience skews younger, and I never want to write something that might scare them. I haven't updated in quite a while because while I'm on the road to recovery, it's never 100% guaranteed, and I feel that proclaiming "I'm cured!" would be jinxing it.

Essentially, I went to college in New York City in Fall 2015. Less than a week in, I caught a cold from my roommate and I didn't get better. I missed several days of class, spent most days sleeping, and barely had enough energy to get something to eat. I went to go spend the afternoon with a family friend, and I was so tired she booked me an emergency appointment with her son's pediatrician. He sent me in for tests at the hospital, and I woke up in the ICU around three weeks later.

At the time, I had a diagnosis of generic pulmonary failure – but it wasn't correct. In order to breathe, they'd given me a tracheostomy. I'd also been tube-fed, so I had lost so much weight that at first I couldn't walk at all. Initially, I wasn't very upset, most likely due to the massive medications I was on that kept me fairly sedated at all times. But I learned I had to go back home to San Francisco and that made me devastated. At home, I started seeing a pulmonologist, got steroid prescriptions, and was allowed to let my trach hole close up. I worked really hard! I still never really had a cut-and-dry diagnosis, but I was on strong daily medications and they seemed to be working. So in fall 2016, I went back to school in New York again.

This time, I lasted longer. I stayed for about a month or so. But things started to fracture: I got three colds; I wasn't thinking clearly; I couldn't do school assignments that, rationally, I knew were easy. Eventually I decided I needed to come home. I felt it was my fault, like I wasn't trying hard enough.

One day, I got a severe headache and vomiting. We went to the emergency room, and they quickly took me in an ambulance to UCSF Hospital. I had severe inflammation in my brain, to the point the doctors were shocked I was even walking. I got discharged around…Christmas, I think? But a few weeks later, the entire left side of my body began to feel numb and tingly, so we went to the hospital as a precaution. They diagnosed me with some sort of brain condition, and put me on a treatment of regular IV drips. But that, too, was incorrect.

One doctor thought: "You know, this isn't adding up." So she surveyed my entire case and realized the inflammation in my lungs was the same thing now clouding my brain. On a hunch, she did a simple blood test and discovered I have an extraordinarily rare genetic disorder: hemophagocytic lymphohistiocytosis (HLH), which more often than not goes undiagnosed because it's so uncommon and has a high mortality rate. For this, there is only one treatment: chemotherapy and a bone marrow transplant. So that's what I had, and I'm on the road to recovery now! I wouldn't say I feel 100% back to normal, but at least my brain is working well enough now that I can read novels again and process the information.

Anyway, it's not a very nice story to tell, which is why I haven't really told it in any Chapel-specific circles. But if anything can come out of my discussing it, I'd hope that it would raise awareness so more doctors might think to test for HLH and other rare hematologic disorders. Many doctors have never seen a case of it in their entire careers!

What's next for Emma T. Capps?

A functional immune system.

How can people find out more about your work?

They can read the entirety of THE CHAPEL CHRONICLES online at www.chapelchronicles.com! It's all there, except for some work I've done for Dark Horse Presents, as I don't own the copyright to those. And the latest for LEAGUE OF FONTS is up on www.leagueoffonts.com – although that's on indefinite hiatus due to the aforementioned health issues, which I feel horrifically guilty about.

Beyond that, I have a Facebook page for THE CHAPEL CHRONICLES, and I'm on Twitter – @EmmaTCapps. On Facebook I've been largely inactive, as I know some younger kids do follow me there, and I've yet to think of a PG-rated way of describing brain surgery. I update my Twitter account slightly more frequently. Previously, I posted solely about my artwork, but lately it's been about my health, books, and taking nice baths (verdict: acceptable for all ages. Don't ever feel like you're too old for a bubble bath. Trust me).

Readers of this blog are more than familiar with my love/appreciation of pie. What's your favorite kind?

That's a tough one, because there are two things I am excellent at baking: pie and chocolate cake, in that order. I haven't specified the pie flavor because I have a good crust recipe and I can usually make them come out equally well. I will say I'm not a big fan of pumpkin pie, so I'd have to say my favorites are probably in the berry territory (berritory?) – I just made a blackberry one, in a desperate culinary plea to woo my new neighbors' affections, so right now that's where I'm leaning. My mom prefers peach, though, so I make those more frequently. Yikes, now I'm hungry…!

Christine Conradt

Originally posted: Mar 1 2019

With more than 70 produced credits, screenwriter/producer/director/author Christine Conradt received her Bachelor's degree in Screenwriting from the esteemed University of Southern California's School of Cinematic Arts and then worked briefly in development and as a reader before launching herself as a successful writer. Christine naturally gravitated to crime dramas and thrillers, and eventually went back to grad school to receive a master's degree in Criminal Justice from Boston University.

Christine's films have aired on Lifetime, LMN, Fox, Showtime, UPtv, Hallmark, and USA. She is the writer behind some of Lifetime's most successful franchises including the "at 17" series, which she turned into a three-book series, published by HarperCollins. She has directed four TV movies and is attached to direct two more this year.

Christine also acts as a script consultant. More information about her services, books, and bio can be found at ChristineConradt.com. She frequently posts tips for writers on her Facebook page. She lives in Los Angeles with her husband and two rescued cats, and in her spare time, loves to travel.

What's the last thing you read or watched that you thought was incredibly well-written?

Does a documentary count? Probably not, but I'll mention it anyway because I found it to be very thought-provoking — THREE IDENTICAL STRANGERS. It's about triplets who were separated at birth and later found each other. I haven't seen a lot of movies this past year because I've been so busy but I did think BIRD BOX was well done for an adaptation.

Sometimes adaptations feel stilted, especially those that take place over a long period of time, but Bird Box didn't feel that way to me. I found myself getting lost in the story which means it was well-written. One of my favorite movies was Vince Gallo's first film— BUFFALO '66. The story is simple and the characters are really well-drawn. I can watch that movie over and over.

Were you always a writer, or was it something you eventually discovered you had a knack for?

I can honestly say it was what I was born to do. I love writing and telling stories. As soon as I could hold a pen, I was writing short stories. I won my first writing award— the Young Author's Award— when I was in the third grade. I grew up in the Midwest in the late 80s/early 90s and at that time, there was no film industry there at all. No film schools, nothing. I didn't know screenwriting existed as a career until I received a brochure from the University of Southern California my junior year of high school and it listed it as a major. If I've ever had an epiphany, it was in that moment. I knew that's what I wanted to do. So I abandoned my plans to go to law school and applied to USC.

How'd you get your start in the industry?

After graduating with a BFA in Screenwriting from USC, I worked briefly in development but didn't like it. I was constantly reading and giving notes on other people's scripts and had to constantly sit with a jealousy that they were doing what I wanted to be doing. I did a rewrite on a USA movie, got fired off that, and didn't get any more writing work for about four years. During that time, I was working at a YMCA as a lifeguard and fitness instructor and they promoted me to Director. Soon after, they promoted me to Senior Director. I was managing million dollars in budgets and supervising about 45 employees. The hours were long and I stopped writing for the most part.

One day, my Executive Director brought me into her office and told me they wanted to promote me to Executive Director of a branch in the neighboring city. The money they were offering was enticing but because of all the training I'd be sent to, they wanted me to give them a five-year commitment. I went home that night and realized I wasn't living the life I was supposed to be living – I was supposed to be a writer. So the next day, I went back and told her that I couldn't accept the job and I was giving my 30-day notice. I took out a loan to live on for six months and decided to spend every day of that period writing. If I couldn't make it happen in six months, I'd go back and get another job at the YMCA, but at least I had given it a shot. Fortunately, during that time, I wrote two screenplays. Neither sold but both got me rewrite work, which turned into more rewrite work, and so on and so on.

At the end of the six months, I was on my way, but I wasn't there yet. So I took a job as an editor for an international publishing company while I continued to intermittently do these rewrites. It was hard to go to script meetings because I had this day job. One day the producer asked me what it would take for me to give up my day job. He was annoyed that I could never come to meetings until 5pm. I told him I needed to make the same amount that the publishing company was paying me and he agreed to give me enough work to cover my lost income. That was the day I started to 'make a living' as writer.

A large percentage of your credits are for TV movies. How much of a difference is there writing for TV (and TV movies) compared to features?

There's a big difference between TV movies and feature films. First, the content can't be as edgy as in a feature and it's much more formulaic. Every network has a brand and when you write for that network, whatever you deliver has to fit within that scope, so in that way, it's more difficult. You have to be creative and original despite all the limitations. The structure is also different. In TV movies, we use an eight or nine act structure (which basically fits into the traditional three act structure) but has three times as many cliffhangers. You have to end on a tension point before a commercial break to keep the audience from flipping the channel. In a theatrical feature, you have a captive audience so the story can unravel more slowly. Theatrical features also tend to be more high concept than TV movies. A lot of people think that a TV movie is just a movie that airs on television. There's a lot more to it than that.

What do you consider the components of a good script?

Probably the same things that most people do. For me, characters are what define a story. Not plot. The best scripts are emotional, not cerebral. They make us think but more importantly, make us feel. The way to accomplish that is with well-defined characters who have plot goals and thematic goals and who choose to struggle for what they want rather than let life simply happen to them. Those are the characters, and consequently, the stories that stay with you long after you leave the theater or turn off the TV

What are some of the most common screenwriting mistakes you see?

Passive characters. The most annoying thing to hear when I ask a writer what her character wants is "He just wants to keep his life the way it is." That's not a goal. A character adverse to change isn't fascinating. I also see a lot of redundancy in scripts. In a screenplay, real estate is precious. You have to write clearly, economically, and infuse that writing with style without being verbose. Over-explaining in both dialogue and action pulls the reader out of the story.

In addition to your TV work, you've also branched out into print with your "at 17" book series. How'd that come about, and how does it compare to writing for a visual medium?

The "at 17" series is a successful franchise on Lifetime Network. It was the brainchild of one of the producers I work with and I've been the primary writer behind those movies for about a decade now. In 2014, I pitched him the idea that we should turn those movies into a YA book series and he championed the idea. Neither of us knew much about the publishing industry so he handed it off to me to figure out. I took the script from MISSING AT 17 which had already aired and wrote it as a manuscript. I went to the Greater Los Angeles Writers Conference and pitched it to an agent there. He read the manuscript and loved it. He ended up partnering with another agent in NYC and they secured a three-book deal with HarperCollins. Harper wanted each book to come out one month apart in the summer and for the last book to align with the premiere of the Lifetime movie with the same title. So in May, June, and July of 2018, MISSING AT 17, PREGNANT AT 17, and MURDERED AT 17 were released.

For me, writing prose is much harder than writing a screenplay. Even though I started out writing prose, I hadn't done it in years. When you're writing a screenplay, you have to 'show' instead of 'tell.' That means you can't write what the characters are thinking or feeling or pondering. In a novel, that's mostly what you do. So I had to retrain myself to move in and out of the characters' thoughts instead of just giving them actions and I had to switch from the omniscient perspective of a screenplay to first person. The books follow multiple characters in first person so that was fun to write. Picking up where one character leaves off and continuing the story with a different character. But it was definitely a challenge.

Follow-up – when can we expect to see the publication of ZOMBIE AT 17?

Ha! The movie ZOMBIE AT 17 premiered on Halloween weekend in 2018 and was a fun take on the "at 17" series. It's about a girl who, after getting bit by a cat, contracts the zombie virus. As she teams up with an alienated guy in her high school who has an obsession with zombies to figure out how to stop the progression of the disease, she witnesses a semi-confession to a murder by one of her boyfriend's friends. When her boyfriend refuses to rat out his friend, she involves herself in the investigation while trying to hide her zombie symptoms from the rest of the world. I don't know if it will ever become a book because it's a bit off-genre, but I think it would make a great one.

What are some key rules/guidelines every writer should know?

- Give your characters goals
- Create obstacles for your characters. Achieving their goals shouldn't be easy.
- Don't obsess on formatting. Focus on writing a good story.
- Read scripts. Lots of scripts. Not just books on how to write screenplays.
- Subplots (or B-stories) need to have some effect on the A-story. If you can cut out the subplot and nothing changes in the A story, you failed.
- Don't judge your characters. Every person feels justified in their actions. Your characters are the same way. To write them, you must believe they're justified as well, even when they do really bad things.
- Write every day. Even if it's only for a half hour. And even if you have writer's block. Professional writers write every day. Train yourself to do the same and pretty soon, you'll

stop having writer's block and you'll be surprised at how easily the writing comes.

What kind of impact or influence has your experience as a writer had on your work as a director or producer?

Some directors come up as cinematographers, some as actors. Coming up as a former writer, I think I pay more attention to how the visuals support the content of the story. I hate stylistic shots for the sake of being stylistic. The best shots are the ones that you don't even realize are shots– because you're so wrapped up in the visual storytelling. I think as a writer, I'm good at letting the moments that need to breathe, breathe. Story is always first. There are lots of visual ways to tell a story. As a director, it's your job to choose the best one.

You've also spoken at a lot of conferences and workshops about screenwriting. Are there any particular points or lessons you make sure to include as part of those?

One thing I mention at every conference is not to compare your journey as a writer to anyone else's. Everyone always wants to know how professional writers broke into the industry, yet they can't emulate it even if they know. It's not like becoming a doctor where you go to med school and do your residency and become a doctor. There are infinite ways to become successful as a writer.

And it depends on your goal. If your goal is to simply make a living writing, you'll make different choices than if your goal is to sell a TV pilot and become a showrunner. Be laser-focused on your goal, but also be flexible enough to take advantage of opportunities even if you aren't sure how they're going to get you there. Sometimes those opportunities turn out to be much better than anything you had planned.

How can people find out more about you and the services you provide?

People can contact me directly through the contact page at christineconradt.com. I'm available to speak and give workshops, and I offer screenplay consulting services as well which are outlined on my website. They can also follow me on Twitter at @CConradt or like my page on Facebook. I post a lot of contests and other opportunities and tips for screenwriters on my FB page.

Readers of this blog are more than familiar with my love/appreciation of pie. What's your favorite kind?

It's a dead heat between blueberry and sour cream raisin.

Barb Doyon/Extreme Screenwriting

Originally posted: May 22 2020

Barb Doyon is the owner/founder of Extreme Screenwriting, a Los Angeles-based screenplay and TV pilot coverage service. She is well known among Hollywood producers as a skilled ghostwriter who is also a produced screenwriter, producer and award-winning documentary writer.

She's a yearly keynote speaker at the Script-to-Screen Summit and has authored books on screenwriting including EXTREME SCREENWRITING: SCREENPLAY WRITING SIMPLIFIED, EXTREME SCREENWRITING: TELEVISION WRITING SIMPLIFIED, TURN YOUR IDEA INTO A HIT REALITY-TV SHOW, 10 WAYS TO GET A HOLLYWOOD AGENT TO CALL YOU! and MAGNETIC SCREENPLAY MARKETING. Before opening Extreme Screenwriting, she worked at Walt Disney Studios writing press releases for the studio and Disney Sports.

What's the last thing you read or watched that you thought was incredibly well-written?

Extreme Screenwriting's client Larry Postel's Netflix movie THE MAIN EVENT was a solid, inspirational read. Larry captured the Follow Your Dreams theme and wove it into a compelling conflict that incited a hero to break through his flaws and become a champion. It's the story of a little boy who takes on WWE Superstars and I love how the trailer states the theme.

How'd you get your start in the industry?

I worked at Walt Disney Studios in the press room where I wrote daily press releases for then-CEO Michael Eisner and the studio's production companies. One day a producer asked if I had time to do coverages and he showed me how to spot the diamonds among the coal heap. This eventually branched into my company Extreme Screenwriting.

What do you consider the components of a good script?

Whether they realize it or not, audiences want to viscerally live through a hero and experience the types of change they can't, won't, or are too afraid to implement in their own lives. Regardless of genre, the writer should make sure that the external and internal conflicts are interlocked, resulting in an external conflict that forces change in a hero. Most writers are excellent at coming up with unique concepts, but fall short when it comes to the hero's flaw and arc. A good script combines external and internal conflicts to solidify a hero's arc.

What are some key rules/guidelines every writer should know?

Interlock internal and external conflicts, as noted above.

A producer should be able to remove all dialogue from a screenplay and still know what the movie is about. It's called a 'motion picture' for a reason.

Don't take format for granted. Learn how to use it to create pacing, emotion and to help guarantee fewer scenes are rewritten or deleted during the development phase.

Stop asking gurus to explain subtext and start listening. Learn to hear subtext in everyday dialogue. This is the fastest, easiest way to learn how to write it and how to become a pro at lingo.

Don't toss in something because you think it's interesting. If Mona's red skirt doesn't mean something to the story as a whole, then leave it out.

Learn the genre rules! Producers buy screenplays based on genre.

Start thinking of description as action and create a moving picture. Don't tell us the room's filthy. Show John walk in, toss cigarettes into an overflowing ashtray and kick his feet up on a pile of yellow newspapers.

Be able to state the screenplay's theme in one line. Producers ask, 'What is the theme?' to weed out amateurs from pros. Amateurs can't answer this question.

Your hero should get the best lines, the last line, the big scene moments, a grand entrance, and the worst-case scenario should happen to them and they alone should resolve the main, external conflict.

What was the inspiration/motivation for your book MAGNETIC SCREENPLAY MARKETING?

It's heartbreaking to see extraordinarily talented, aspiring screenwriters struggle for years to get a producer to read their material. Extreme Screenwriting does help writers promote their material in our monthly newsletter, but writers need to spend as much time marketing as they do writing. Most do not! Instead, they send out a few queries here and there, maybe attend a pitch festival every couple of years and that's it.

The market is rapidly changing, and if aspiring screenwriters don't change with it, they'll be left behind with little hope of getting their material into the right hands. The change in the industry requires a new way of thinking and it does have a learning curve, so that's why I decided to make a book detailing how to get ahead of the curve and beat the competition with this marketing strategy.

This book is very different from other screenwriting books in that it focuses more on what a writer can do AFTER they've gained some experience and have market-ready scripts. Is what you describe a newer development for screenwriters, and what results have you seen from it?

The marketing technique I outlined in the book, related to getting a producer to call you, isn't new to the industry. It's been around for a long time, but until recently, this strategy hasn't applied to screenwriters. However, there's been a shift in the industry. Like any other product (yes, a screenplay is a product), the buyer (producer) wants social proof of its viability and is even hiring staff to find material with this 'proof' attached.

The MAGNETIC SCREENPLAY MARKETING book teaches the writer how to develop this marketing strategy and put it to use. Prior to publishing the book, I worked with 13 writers to beta test the strategy resulting in agent representation, three options, a television pilot deal and 362 combined read requests, averaging 27 per beta tester. A few did fail at the process, but they didn't complete the steps, skipped steps, or simply quit before even giving it a try. Therefore, results will vary, but the bottom line is the fact that the industry is changing. I highly recommend aspiring writers get aboard this fast-moving train before they're left behind.

One portion of the book is about writers obtaining "bread and butter assignments". What does that mean, and why are they a potential avenue for writers?

This pertains to one of the strategies outlined in a section of the book on how to get an agent to call you. The first agent 99% of writers sign with will be from a boutique agency. These are the smaller agencies in town and while they do make sales, most of their commissions are generated from writing assignments, rewrites, and ghostwriting. It's so prevalent that it's literally become their 'bread and butter', in other words it's the main moneymaker.

However, a lot of writers refuse to do this type of work. They'd rather wait around to sell their own screenplays. This sounds reasonable, but if it's been a year (or two) and a writer's work hasn't sold and the writer won't do this lucrative work, they become dead weight for the agent. This creates an 'opening' for the aspiring writer who notes in queries that they're open to all kinds of writing assignments! During the beta test, one of our writers gained representation using this strategy. A writer who isn't open to doing assignments is leaving a lot of cash on the table and missing out on a golden opportunity to gain representation.

You mention sending in writing samples (when and only when requested). One of the options you suggest is to send the last 10 pages of a script. Why the last 10 as opposed to the first 10, and what results have you (or writers who've done this) seen from this?

This is a strategy I decided to add to the book after several years of hearing of its success. Most agents, producers and story analysts agree that most writers know how to nail Act I, but then the material starts to fall apart. The result is an accumulation of story points that miss the mark.

Therefore, if a writer can still intrigue them with a strong ending that reveals voice, theme, solidifies a plot, and nails down pacing while intriguing them to want to know more, then the screenplay's worth reading. This isn't the preference for all agents and producers, but even those who start off requesting the entire screenplay often flip to the end first.

You also have a section of the book regarding writers creating teaser trailers for their scripts. What's a teaser trailer for a script, and what's the advantage in doing it?

This is part of the new marketing strategy that involves creating an audience for a screenplay via social media, primarily YouTube. This doesn't involve a Hollywood-style trailer, but rather a simple teaser video that can literally be done for $0 cost (the book shows how) and all the writer has to do is write a 1-page script.

Think about it. For years, producers have purchased books and reality-TV concepts that got their start on social media, based solely on the fact they came with a built-in audience. When a writer sits down to pitch a script, I guarantee the producer is wondering if the story can draw an audience, but imagine the potential for a sale if the writer walks in the door with an audience already attached to the screenplay. It's a huge advantage and can make the project a hot commodity!

How can people find out more about you and the services you provide?

Extreme Screenwriting invites writers to visit us at www.ExtremeScreenwriting.com. We offer coverage, a free monthly newsletter, and see the Bookshelf tab for the Magnetic Screenplay Marketing book (available for instant eBook download).

I also have three new books, all available on Amazon:

SCREENPLAY FORMAT: LEARN HOW TO FORMAT LIKE A PRO
Teaches screenwriters industry format from basics to pro techniques, including how to use format to create emotion, suspense, etc.

SCREENPLAY NOTEBOOK: STORY ANALYST'S CHECKLIST

A workbook that includes Story Analyst's Checklist for plot/execution, characters, dialogue and scenes with 26 blank pages for each section to work through problem areas. Makes a great keepsake.

SCREENWRITERS WORLD: WORD SEARCH PUZZLE BOOK
Great for breaking writer's block and having fun. Makes a great gift for screenwriters.

Readers of this blog are more than familiar with my love/appreciation of pie. What's your favorite kind?

Homemade blueberry.

Brooks Elms

Originally posted: Feb 7 2020

Brooks Elms is a WGA screenwriter of 25+ scripts with a specialty of crafting grounded personal characters and gut-punch story tension. He's currently rewriting an Oscar-winning writer. Brooks also loves coaching fellow writers who have a burning ambition to deeply serve their audiences: www.brookselms.com

What's the last thing you read or watched that you thought was incredibly well-written?

JOKER. Because it's difficult to build empathy for protagonists with flaws that lead to violence against innocent people, especially with all the mass shootings these days. I have ethical questions about whether this was a worthy screenplay to produce because the film can't help but celebrate what it's also trying to condemn. And I suspect it will inspire as many (if not more) negative consequences as positive ones – but that makes the screenwriting all the more impressive and skillful. Because this was a very popular film and the bar was VERY high for that level of success.

How'd you get your start in the industry?

Making movies with my friends in high school, which led to NYU film school, then writing, directing and producing indie features. In the last decade, I've mostly focused on screenwriting. In between my writing assignments, I taught a screenwriting class at UCLA Extension for a while and now I coach other ambitious writers working at the intermediate to professional levels, as my own schedule allows.

Is recognizing good writing something you think can be taught or learned?

What's the alternative theory – that people come out of the womb knowing how to write well? It's a matter of defining what you love about other stories and getting familiar with the craft choices that lead to those results. I teach this to everybody from beginners to veteran writers so…. yup.

What do you consider the components of a good script?

It's about the harmony between components. The craft is taking elements (premise, hero, goal, conflict, structure, relationships, setting, theme, tone, etc..) and adjusting aspects of them (size, shape, style, amount, etc..) until we find the right collective balance which allows something bigger to speak through the parts.

What are some of the most common screenwriting mistakes you see?

Losing touch with the delight of the process. And stopping because of that.

What story tropes are you just tired of seeing?

Every trope has the potential to be powerful if created with authenticity. It only feels cliche when there's too much emotional distance from the truth of the intention.

What are some key rules/guidelines every writer should know?

I stay away from language choices like "every writer should know X". Those types of words can be a distraction from listening to the subtle impulses of your voice. Instead, I invite people to follow their passion. What excites us about our current story? How can we play with elements to unleash more of that excitement? When we share material for feedback, what's blocking other people from deeper levels of excitement? "Confusion" is the most common blockage followed by "tepid goals and conflicts."

Have you ever read a spec script that was an absolute, without-a-doubt "recommend"? If so, what were the reasons why?

The Duffer Brothers' HIDDEN, which they wrote before STRANGER THINGS. It was a masterful display of milking tension using minimal assets in a scene. I used that script to teach myself how to make a huge impact on the way I write tension.

How do you feel about screenwriting contests? Worth it or not?

ALL the paths toward advancing your career have you pitted against the odds. So just pick the paths that speak to you and your budget. Contests can certainly be helpful so have fun playing that game, and detach from the outcomes. It's about enjoying the journey and welcoming those that come along that happen to love your work as much as you do.

How can people find out more about you and the services you provide?

Check out www.brookselms.com

I run a few programs for writers looking to cross milestones as fast as humanly possible, in ways that are effortless and fun. One program is a deep dive 1:1 mentorship that's very exclusive and competitive to get into. And I have other ways of helping writers too. So if writers enjoy the content they've seen from me online, I suggest they reach out because my team will be happy to help, in one way or another.

Readers of this blog are more than familiar with my love/appreciation of pie. What's your favorite kind?

Now we're getting to the essential question. The answer is pecan. It's rich, heavenly and it shines beneath a scoop of vanilla ice cream. Shout out to banana cream for a close second place. It can be spectacular when it's baked well, but breaks my heart when it's often messed up.

Jimmy George/Script Butcher

Originally posted: July 28 2017

Jimmy George, aka Script Butcher, has been writing and producing films for over a decade. Along with optioning several screenplays, Jimmy has lent his name as co-writer/co-producer to six award winning feature-length films, garnering rave reviews, and boasting international distribution.

He has a talent for engineering fun and innovative productions on shoe-string budgets with few of the modern technological marvels used in major Hollywood blockbusters. Each of his films have been praised for circumventing their meager budgets, standing out through memorable storytelling.

Jimmy co-wrote and co-produced WNUF HALLOWEEN SPECIAL (2013), which won numerous festival awards, alongside national press from The New York Times, VICE, MTV, Birth.Movies.Death, Fandango, and Red Letter Media, and is currently available on the AMC Networks' streaming service, Shudder.

After tearing up the festival circuit, his film CALL GIRL OF CTHULHU generated enormous buzz in the horror industry. Harry Knowles of Aintitcoolnews.com declared it "fun, better than it should be and quite splattacular.".

Jimmy's seventh feature, WHAT HAPPENS NEXT WILL SCARE YOU, will be released next year.

In addition to writing and producing, Jimmy has a passion for helping creators succeed. As the Script Butcher, he consults with screenwriters, empowering them with the necessary tools to sharpen their scripts into dynamic stories that slice through the competition.

What's the last thing you read/watched that you thought was incredibly well-written?

The pilot episode for GLOW. The world-building is excellent. It takes you into a sub-culture that's mysterious and relatively unknown. The characters are memorable and entertaining. We meet the lead character at her lowest point. It leaves us with so much promise for what could take place during the series. Does everything a pilot should do and more.

How'd you get your start reading scripts?

There are many screenwriting gurus out there. I am not one of them. I'm just a guy who's written a ton of screenplays, produced a half-dozen movies of my own, and learned a lot along the way.

Over the last ten years of making movies, I've become the go-to script doctor for a lot of friends and colleagues. I've been doing this for free for a decade and it became clear a few years ago that this was my purpose. So I decided to start this service and try to make a living doing what I love.

Telling stories is what I was put on this Earth to do. Helping others fine tune their stories is a close second. I've been in your shoes. I know the blood, sweat, and tears it takes to complete a screenplay. This isn't a job for me. It's my passion. It's what I live for.

Where does the moniker "Script Butcher" come from?

Whenever someone would ask for notes, I always delivered their script covered with red ink. The pages looked bloody. I once joked with a friend that I was their "script butcher" and it just stuck. To this day, every time I finish a set of notes my hands are covered with red ink splatters. I have a background in horror so a lot of people assume those are the only scripts I work with, but I provide the same exhaustive notes for all genres. I'd say 75% of my clients don't write horror.

Is recognizing good writing something you think can be taught or learned?

Writing well and recognizing good writing are skills that go hand in hand. Both can be taught and learned. For me, recognizing good writing as compared to bad has come from reading thousands of scripts at all levels of the talent spectrum. Having my own scripts brought to life on a frequent basis, sitting in theaters watching what works and doesn't has also taught me invaluable lessons most script doctors haven't had the opportunity to learn or pass along.

Studying the work of pros is a must too, but a lot of scripts available to the public are shooting drafts which are different from spec scripts and teach new writers bad lessons. So much can be learned from script consultants as well. I wouldn't be where I am today without the mentoring advice and guidance I received from my own trusted script doctors.

I didn't go to film school. The notes I received from these professionals over the course of a decade and a half, became my film school. By failing time and again, by continuing to experiment with the form and seeking constant feedback, I learned the craft. I never stopped trying to get better. Growing thick skin and learning how to use feedback to improve your stories is an important skill set for a writer.

Sending my scripts for notes became a crucial part of the writing process and continues to be.

What are the components of a good script?

A good script should have an original, marketable concept. With flawed relatable characters who are actively seeking something they care deeply about, that we can emotionally connect with and root for, and that deals with the most important events of these character's lives.

It should present a visual goal for the character or characters to achieve which form the central story question, and present primal, relatable stakes for what will happen if they fail to achieve those visual goals with formidable forces of antagonism that cause never-ending complications, standing in the way of the character's achieving their goals.

It's properly formatted on the page, relies on visuals instead of dialogue to tell the story, with plausible surprises and reversals of expectation at every turn.

And it builds to an emotionally satisfying climax that answers the central story question of whether our characters will achieve their visual goal in a positive or negative manner.

Other elements such as a quick pace, character arcs, thematic resonance, and memorable dialogue are a bonus, but not absolutely necessary for a script to do its job.

(Some of this is inspired by Terry Rossio's 60 Question Checklist, which every screenwriter should read.)

What are some of the most common mistakes you see?

FAILURE TO DELIVER ON THE PROMISE OF THE PREMISE. A story is a promise. Imagine MRS. DOUBTFIRE if the story followed Robin Williams working as an accountant instead of following the trials and tribulations of trying to reconnect with his wife and kids while dressed as an old woman.

The audience is waiting for you to deliver on the promise of your concept. If your script is about killer beer, you better have a beer pong massacre scene.

TONAL IMBALANCE. If you're writing SCHINDLER'S LIST, there's no room for campy comedy. Vice versa. Even if you're mixing genres, keep your characters' reactions to the events around them and the events themselves consistent in tone.

LACK OF CLARITY EMOTIONAL OR OTHERWISE. Clarity of what a character is feeling in reaction to a situation or what is being conveyed in general is a common issue I encounter with client scripts. Because the story is alive in your head, it's difficult to tell what is and isn't conveyed on the page. It's all crystal clear for the writer, but often muddled on the page.

There are many more common mistakes, but these are the big ones.

What story tropes are you just tired of seeing?

UNDESERVED CELEBRITY STATUS. I see so many scripts that give their characters a level of celebrity status that's unbelievable simply for the sake of telling the media-frenzied story they're trying to tell. The paparazzi and press are very specific about the types of people they will follow. Make sure your characters are worthy of the celebrity status you're giving them in your story.

USING NEWSPAPER HEADLINES AS EXPOSITION. Many of my clients rely on one newspaper headline after another to show the passage of time and relay important exposition. Media has changed. This is an antiquated story device that no longer holds weight with the audience.

What are the 3 most important rules every writer should know?

REVERSE EXPECTATION at every turn in a way that feels organic to the story and not calculated or contrived.

FIND THE CLICHE AND THROW IT AWAY. If we've seen it or heard it before, find another way to show it or say it that's premise-specific. This will ensure your story always feels fresh and unique. Premise specificity is the key to storytelling freshness.

MAKE IT VISUAL. If dialogue comes last instead of first when you're crafting scenes, it will ensure your story is cinematic and not better suited for the stage.

Have you ever read a script that was an absolute, without-a-doubt "recommend"? If so, could you give the logline?

I have once, it's called BASATAI by my longtime client Suzan Battah. She's in the process of turning it into a graphic novel. You can find out more here. https://www.patreon.com/suzanbattah

How do you feel about screenwriting contests? Worth it or not?

Not worth it. Writers put so much time, emphasis, and worst of all, money into contests. In my opinion they'd be better off spending that time improving their craft and spending their money on attending networking events and writing workshops.

While I understand the allure of getting a festival or contest win to stand out from the crowd of writers trying to break in, a contest win can be detrimental to a writer's sense of skill level and give them a false sense of completion with their scripts.

I've worked with dozens of screenplays that were "award-winning" with multiple festival monikers to their name, that I don't feel would get a RECOMMEND from a single studio reader.

Writers are paying money to contests, being assured their scripts are good enough, when they aren't ready yet. There's nothing more detrimental to your career than trying to shop around a script that isn't ready.

How can people get in touch with you to find out more about the services you provide?

My website has all the details you'll need at www.scriptbutcher.com/services. You can also find me on Twitter at www.twitter.com/scriptbutcher, Instagram at www.instagram.com/_jimmygeorge and Facebook at www.facebook.com/scriptbutcher

Readers of this blog are more than familiar with my love/appreciation of pie. What's your favorite kind?

Offbeat answer here. My wife and I were passing through Intercourse, Pennsylvania, otherwise known as Amish country. There was a gift shop that sold shoofly pie with cartoonish construction paper flies advertising how fresh it was. We bought a slice. Needless to say, it was so delicious we left with two whole pies.

Lisa Gomez

Originally posted: Jan 31 2020

Lisa Gomez is a Los Angeles-based screenwriter, novelist, songwriter and a professional story analyst for The Black List. They write screenplays, songs and novels with their twin sister. Together, the twin siblings have placed in the Top 50 of the Academy Nicholl Fellowships in Screenwriting and are represented by Empirical Evidence.

The twins are working on 3 original pilots; a 30-minute dark comedy involving an asexual lead character, a biopic drama pilot in the vein of THE QUEEN'S GAMBIT and a female-driven SHERLOCKian-inspired pilot. Lisa is currently obsessed with Marvel, Disneyland, matcha, and reading as many books and comic books as they possibly can.

What was the last thing you read/watched you considered to be extremely well-written?

The pilot of BARRY. It has everything that makes a story compelling and unique. Professional screenwriters have always given aspiring screenwriters these three bits of advice when setting up a character and a world: 1) Start the story with your main character doing something interesting. 2) Show the main character's day to day, show the audience what a typical day in the life of this main character looks like. 3) Show the audience the main character's problem. Well, in a whopping 30 minutes, this show delivers all of this and sets up the promise for more.

[Spoilers for the pilot of BARRY ahead]. The very first moment of the show shows Barry walk into a hotel room, holding a gun while the camera mostly focuses on the dead body that's lying on a bed with a bullet through his head. Immediately, this sets up the main character doing something interesting... okay, so, he's a killer. Possibly a hitman. Whoa, that's interesting. Then, it shows Barry's day-to-day. We see him fly home on an airplane, get annoyed at a fellow passenger that opens a window to let the light in (a subtle but effective metaphor), then he plays video games, alone, and takes a shower, alone. Immediately, we get it. This is one lonely and depressed dude that gets no fulfillment from killing.

So, within the first five minutes (and theoretically the first five pages of a screenplay), Barry sets up the main character doing something interesting (killing someone), shows the main character's typical day to day (he flies home after a hit, he's alone, bored and does nothing substantial besides killing) and sets up what his problem is (that he's depressed and gets no fulfillment from his job). It's a pitch-perfect setup to a show. One could argue that the set-up is traditional and therefore cliché. But because this is a unique character and the premise is so bizarre, Bill Hader and Alec Berg made this setup interesting and makes the audience clamoring for more. And this is all just the first five minutes... if you haven't seen this show, please do. It's a masterclass in writing.

One of your job titles is story analyst. What does that job entail, and what are your responsibilities?

A story analyst is essentially someone who gives script coverage for studios, production companies and agencies. In other words, someone who receives a script and has to write notes on that script, on what's working and what's not working with the script, if I would pass, consider or recommend the script for the agency/studio/company. I have to read the script in its entirety, write a synopsis of the script, write a logline, describe the main characters and then write comments on why I would pass or recommend the script. Occasionally, in my notes, I offer solutions to story problems.

How'd you get your start doing that?

This is a fun story. My sister actually found an internship listing for a script coverage reader for a literary agency on entertainmentcareers.net. I applied and got the job. I did that for about a year. Then, as luck would have it, a Nicholl fellow walked into my retail job and I recognized him because he spoke at one of the classes that I took at UCLA Extension. We got to talking and he said he could refer me to a low-paying but highly regarded script coverage job. I applied, had to do test notes on a script and then got that job.

Once I started getting more and more experience, I had screenwriting friends I'd met in various networking events in LA refer me to different script coverage jobs. Every friend I met through networking was an aspiring screenwriter that eventually got a job in the entertainment industry and either reached out to me about the script coverage job or I would ask if they knew about any script coverage jobs. This is truthfully the first time I finally understood the importance of networking in this city.

When you're reading a script, what about it indicates to you that "this writer really gets it (or doesn't get it)"?

First and foremost, the grammar. I know, that seems like such an obvious answer but it's true. You would not believe how many scripts I read that have beyond atrocious spelling and grammar. Sometimes the ends of sentences don't have periods. I wish I was joking.

Secondly, clarity. What do I mean by that? Clarity is probably the easiest and the hardest aspect of writing a great screenplay. Easy because once you put on the page exactly what you want the reader to know, you're done. Hard because putting exactly what you mean on the page is very very difficult. This is why script coverage or having someone read your script is helpful. It can point out the areas that the writer thinks makes sense but in reality, it doesn't and it only makes sense to the writer.

Clarity, for me, means a few things. One, that the writing makes sense. For example, if you're writing an action scene, please write description that is easy to follow and easy to read. The worst thing you can do for a script reader is make them read lines of description a few times in order to understand what's going on. We get bored and frustrated.

Secondly, that the character's arcs, story and plot is clear. It sounds simple, but again, most scripts don't have this. I think it's because the writer knows the story so well that the writer forgets to put in important and obvious things. For example, I was doing coverage on this script where the main character was queer. It was a very interesting main character, but I didn't understand why this character's queerness affected their journey because every character that interacted with this character loved and relished their identity. The writer then told me "Oh, because this story takes place in 2010." BAM! I now understand the context of the story. But that date was nowhere in the script. It could be little details like that that can make a script clear or unclear.

What do you consider the components of a good script?

Clarity/conciseness. No one wants to read a script that doesn't make sense, or rambles on too long. Make it sweet and to the point. And make it fun and interesting to read.

An interesting main character that has an interesting and relatable problem. So many scripts I read don't have this in its entirety. Especially the relatable part. The main character might have an interesting problem, but it's something that literally no one on this earth can relate to.

When the main character has a goal that's actually attainable, but also difficult. This is something I don't see all the time. What's really important is that your main character has the skills to defeat their problem/the antagonist but it's still difficult.

A great example of this not happening is STAR WARS: THE RISE OF SKYWALKER. Sure, you know that Rey is strong, but you don't know specifically how Rey will be able to defeat Palpatine. This makes the story boring because the audience can't participate in her journey in how she can do that. She just defeats Palpatine. It's not set up how she can. It just happens. This is story suicide.

The script is great if it has something to say. What is your theme? What is your unique point of view on the world? Not only that, but what is your unique point of view on a specific theme? For example, everyone writes about redemption, but what are you trying to specifically say about redemption? Are you saying it's not possible (BARRY), that it is possible, but a very hard road (BOJACK HORSEMAN), or are you saying that it is possible (STAR WARS: RETURN OF THE JEDI)?

Interesting situations/scenes. If you have a scene where two people argue, that can be boring. If you have a scene with two people arguing in the middle of a mall, that instantly makes it more interesting.

Great dialogue. If you have dialogue I've heard before, that makes me cringe. If you have dialogue specific to the character and only that character can say it, it makes me happy.

What are some of the most common screenwriting mistakes you see?

The way screenwriters describe women as beautiful, sexy, or simply defined by their looks. It's disgusting, objectifying and just plain terrible. It's 2020. Women have always been complex. It's time to write us as such.

Too much description. Description writing is very hard, but please don't have paragraphs and paragraphs of description. Try to write what only needs to be in the script but as simply and concisely as possible.

Cliché dialogue. A lot of the scripts I read have the following lines: "It's too late!" "You really don't get it, do you?" "Hi, my name is [blank]." "So, are you new around here?" It's exhausting. We get it. You've seen a lot of movies. Please prove it by not giving us these lines that we've all heard a million times. Sometimes it's inevitable. You have to. But please try to the least you possibly can.

What story tropes are you just tired of seeing?

One-dimensional women. I promise you, women are human beings that have ambitions and feelings that don't revolve around men.

What are some key rules/guidelines every writer should know?

- Write from the heart.
- Write with something to say.
- Get your first draft out as quickly as possible.
- Even if you don't like outlining, do it.
- Read screenplays. They'll help you write screenplays.
- Live life.
- Enjoy the process of writing.
- Show your writing to people who will give you honest feedback.
- Have a clear structure in your story.
- Pitch your show/movie idea to your friends. If they don't like it, either fix what's wrong with the premise or think of another idea.

Screenwriting contests. Worth it or not?

Yes. Contests are great for deadlines and keeping yourself accountable. Because, if you're paying that submission fee, you want to submit the best work that you have. However, don't make your entire screenwriting identity about contests. I did and that got me nowhere. Use them for deadlines and don't think about them after you submit. Just write the next script.

Follow-up: You've placed in the top 50 of the Nicholl. What was the script about, and what happened for you and/or the script as a result?

The Academy Nicholl Fellowships in Screenwriting are amazing. I've had friends become Nicholl Fellows and I've had friends in the top 50. We all have similar experiences.

That script was co-written with my writing partner, my twin sister. It's a biopic about the nine weeks that Vincent van Gogh spent with fellow artist and rival Paul Gauguin. What started off as a friendly rivalry between them ended with Vincent cutting his ear off. It was my sister's and I's first screenplay… and it was the first draft. When we were announced in the top 50, we got about a dozen e-mails from huge agencies… I'm talking, CAA, WME, Anonymous Content, you name it… we sent them our script and then… crickets. I believe this script wasn't ready and I also don't think we sent them out to the agents and managers that would respond to our type of script anyway.

Here's my biggest piece of advice if you place highly in a reputable script contest: contact the managers and agents you want to or agents that represent writers that write similar scripts to you. If my sister and I did that, I think we would have been represented by now.

How can people find out more about you and the services you provide?

Due to an ever-expanding list of projects, I've had to suspend my script consulting services.

Readers of this blog are more than familiar with my love/appreciation of pie. What's your favorite kind?

Aye, there's the rub. Unfortunately, I have a gluten and lactose intolerance, so I can't have pie unless it's gluten-free and dairy-free. I know, it's a sad existence. However, if I could have any pie, I personally love apple pie. Maybe because when my stomach could handle those pesky ingredients, I would always love getting apple pies from McDonald's during my youth and that taste just brings back good, happy childhood memories.

Philip E. Hardy/The Script Gymnasium

Originally posted: Mar 17 2017

Phillip E. Hardy is a four-time optioned screenwriter who also runs The Script Gymnasium script consultancy. His work has recently been presented to Jay Roach, William Morris Endeavor, Tyler Perry Productions and A&E Network. He has placed and won at 45 film festivals and contests including Page International, Austin Film Festival, Cannes Screenplay, Shore Scripts, Screencraft, Beverly Hills Film Festival and Sunscreen Film Festival.

Today's post stems from a discussion between Phillip and myself regarding the benefits and drawbacks of posting your script on a hosting site or taking a more proactive role and doing the work yourself.

You've had some experience with both handling your own material and hosting sites. Do you find one to be more effective than the other, or is it more of a case-by-case basis?

I've had varying degrees of success with different hosting sites. But it's a total crapshoot, especially with paid hosting and pitching sites. One of my colleagues swears by Virtual Pitchfest (VPF). And, at 10 bucks a pop for a pitch, they look attractive to writers on a budget. I've done ten pitches at VPF and though I received some very good feedback on one of my period piece dramas, nobody at that website has requested a script read.

When I first started out, I used Project Greenlight (PG), which was expensive and the responses I received were very sloppy and unprofessional. I did get one read request from a video game company. But I would never use PG again. I know of nobody who has scored with them.

Don't ask me about the Black List. Okay, I'll tell you. I hate them and everything they stand for. However, if you wish to pay their reviewers (frustrated writers with their own axe to grind) seventy five dollars a pop to review your script, then that's the site for you.

International Screenwriters' Association is fairly inexpensive for a premium listing. However, anyone that uses them can call themselves a producer or director. I've made several connections there but they led me nowhere and have netted no financial remuneration.

I've also hooked up with a few folks on Craigslist (CL), which can be a real pain and you have to answer a lot of adds to get any action. One of the best connections I made on CL was with one of the stars of the TNT show "Falling Skies". So you never know who you're talking to but you should vet them out before sending them your scripts.

I've had my best luck at InkTip, which allows you to list a script for four months at a price of sixty dollars for four months. Producers at InkTip shop loglines and will read your summary or request a script read if they're interested in your spec material. For example, I had multiple logline reads today and two of them read the synopsis as well. However, a lot of InkTip clients troll loglines and do little else. I've had a number of script downloads, which have also netted zippo.

However, the InkTip Newsletter has been much more effective for me. The price is the same as the listing. The difference is you can pitch producers looking for specific genres and concepts. I've also written pitches for these clients, which led to a script option and three right-to-shop agreements with a producer that got my work into the hands of some big time production companies and cable networks. I've also bullshitted people and told them I had scripts I hadn't written yet. And then banged them out in a week. This method is not for the faint of heart.

I'm sure most writers know that Amazon Studios has an open door policy about submitting television and feature screenplays. Unfortunately, that door leads to oblivion. And if you can locate one unproduced writer that has something produced by Amazon, I'll buy you lunch at my local Sonic drive-thru. Several months back, I did some research on this and could find no unproduced writers who have made it out of development purgatory. And by unproduced, I mean you've never had a big budget movie made from one of your screenplays.

Lastly, I've used Stage 32 for paid pitch sessions and gotten script requests from four major players including Ridley Scott Productions and Good Fear Management. But if you do a written pitch, you better make sure your logline is catchy, your synopsis is clear and concise and you include the character arc for your protagonist.

The bottom line is use any means possible to get your work into the hands of people you are looking to make movies.

If you're going the DIY route, what methods have worked for you?

Smack-talkin', bold action has worked best for me. I hooked up with several producers looking for projects by telling them I had scripts already written about things they were looking for, including a story about Michael Rockefeller, who disappeared in the Papuan Islands more than fifty years ago. In this particular instance, the producer was advertising and I wrote a logline and synopsis in three hours and pitched it to the guy. He optioned the screenplay I wrote in six days.

In another instance, I did the same thing with another producer looking for an Angela Davis screenplay. However, when the producer asked me if I had a script, I said "sure, it's sitting on the shelf with my screenplays about Huey Newton and Eldridge Cleaver." He got the joke and we wound up working together on several different projects. The DIY Method should include whoring your wares at any given moment and making as many connections as you can. Also, make friends with writers like Paul Zeidman.

Never heard of him. Keeping that theme going, what do you recommend when it comes to using hosting sites?

Passive hosting sites where you don't aggressively work the leads may be a waste of time. Just listing a script without supporting efforts offers little chance for anything happening to further your career.

What's your opinion of hosting sites overall?

If you're not living in Hollywood and getting meetings with producers, hosting sites, along with promoting yourself vigorously and IMHO, competing in film festivals and script contests to relentlessly build your brand, can be a very useful tool to get you access to producers and agents.

As a direct result of hosting sites, I've had material read by A & E, History Channel, Emmett Furla, William Morris Endeavor, Jay Roach, Tyler Perry Productions, Ridley Scott Productions, Zero Gravity, Good Fear Management, Zane W. Levitt and many others.

After putting your script on a hosting site, what should you NOT do?

Don't nag the contacts you make.

Don't be a pain in the ass if someone's interested in your work.

As an experienced writer, what tips would you like to pass along?

If you're a delicate, sensitive woodland creature, then screenwriting isn't for you.

Learn to suck up constant rejection. Never spend more than a few hours wallowing in rejection or failure. Remember, opinions are like assholes, everyone has one. With each setback, learn how to sally forth with renewed vigor.

The best cure for rejection is writing; particularly if it's better writing.

Sometimes a script just sucks. Everyone thinks they have a great idea for a script. More often than not, they're wrong. Sometimes a script just sucks, no matter how many times you rewrite it. Therefore, don't attach yourself to any one effort too much. It may take writing fifty scripts before you find something that really resonates with readers.

If you see writing scripts as a path to riches and fame, you may wish to consider other options.

There ain't no such thing as writers block. There are only writers that write and ones that don't. Look at Bukowski. Drunk or sober, he did great work every day of his life.

Writers who build relationships, maintain their humility and help their colleagues will do better than ones who don't.

If you keep losing script contests, then write better scripts until you win one.

Read books, take classes, seminars, and good advice about scriptwriting and then march to your own creative drummer. If I listened to every asshole who told me I couldn't do something, I'd never accomplish anything.

What are some absolute "Do NOTs"?

Don't tell anyone "this is my first script". But don't think you'll set the world on fire by writing one script.

Don't write something because you think it will have commercial appeal. Write something you believe in.

Don't worry about what everyone else is doing. Endeavor to be an original.

Don't ever rest on your laurels. Keep writing until it becomes second nature AND you can produce even under the most adverse or stressful conditions. You may one day have a job that presents you with just that set of conditions.

Readers of this blog are more than familiar with my love/appreciation of pie. What's your favorite kind?

A good apple pie with a scoop of vanilla ice cream.

Heidi Hornbacher/PageCraft

Originally posted: Dec 11 2020

A graduate of UCLA's screenwriting program, Heidi Hornbacher has written numerous features, treatments, and TV pilots for various independent producers. She's judged for the Slamdance Film Festival screenwriting contest and co-founded the Slamdance Script Clinic. She and her husband founded PageCraft Writing in 2008, offering script coaching and writing retreats in LA and Italy. Her clients include Emmy winners, TV legends, and brand new writers too. Heidi has written, directed, and produced numerous commercials, music videos, and electronic press kits for various artists. She's currently making a documentary film about British artist Paul Whitehead.

What's the last thing you read/watched you considered to be exceptionally well-written?

There is so much great TV right now. I was mesmerized by I MAY DESTROY YOU. Anything that makes me say "wow, I could not have written that" I love. I had a Kenyan writer on my podcast recently and she noted that it was a very African storytelling style which I found particularly interesting.

How'd you get your start in the industry?

I moved to Los Angeles to go to the UCLA Professionals Program in Screenwriting at night and landed a day job at Paramount as a president's assistant. From there it was a lot of reading, learning, developing skills, and networking. And just making things without waiting for permission.

Is recognizing good writing something you think can be taught or learned?

I think this is absolutely something that can be taught. If you have a natural instinct it helps but you can train your eye to spot things the same way a sommelier trains to spot subtle flavor differences in wine. When I first started reading for contests I would decide to advance or decline a script based on instinct, but had to develop the facility to be able to say why.

Once I could point to things like unmotivated dialogue, a major story turn being on the B story but missing from the A story, unearned reveals, etc. it helped me codify those elements into my own writing and into a teachable curriculum for PageCraft.

What do you consider the components of a good script?

Solid characters that have been well developed with clear goals, and positive and negative stakes to achieving those goals. Scenes that work hard to move your story forward and don't just sit there. Even in a reflective moment, we should be learning something new about the character or they should be learning something about themselves. Every scene having a clear Goal-Obstacle-Outcome, or what we call GOO structure. Yes. EVERY SCENE.

What are some of the most common screenwriting mistakes you see?

Where to begin? The most offensive mistakes are things like not spellchecking (how hard is that?) and grammar errors. Those tell me you just don't care about your craft or my time, so why should I give my time to looking at your craft?

A lot of scripts that are findable online, etc. are shooting scripts rather than original scripts so I see a lot of bad habits writers pick up from those such as writing in edit and camera direction. There should never be a CUT TO or CLOSE UP ON in your original script. Every slug line implies a cut so there's that, and you should be able to imply the angle and type of shot by how masterfully you work your action lines.

I see a lot of over-directing the actor from the page. Unless a movement is key to the plot, don't tell your actors how to move their bodies. The hardest thing about screenwriting is getting your head around the fact that it's a collaborative art where we often never meet our collaborators because they come in after we've done our part. Learning to trust that your actors are going to bring nuance and physical choices to the role can be like a trust fall. If you've written the script well with clear context for what that character is going through, the actor will run with it.

What story tropes are you just tired of seeing?

Aside from lazy things like the detective with the board full of photos connected by red string, I'm really tired of societal tropes; rape as a motivator for why a female character becomes stronger, stories that only view Black characters as suffering characters. Can we move on? We're more nuanced as humans so our stories should be too.

Then there are just overused dialogue lines like "it might just work", "that went well", and "we're a lot alike, you and I." We actually have a PowerPoint with stills from over 40 films and shows illustrating how overused that last one is.

What are some key rules/guidelines every writer should know?

As I said above: Make sure there is GOO (Goal-Obstacle-Outcome) in every single scene.

Make sure you have a solid structure and outline before you start writing. You need a roadmap!

Make sure you've done your character work and understand what motivates them. Make sure you've done as much work for the antagonist as for the protagonist so the struggle is worth your protagonist's time.

Make sure every major story turn occurs on the A storyline – the external story. Turns on the B and C storylines can serve as point and counterpoint to that but if a turn is missing from the A story, the narrative will feel off and it can be hard to see why.

Remember that a script is a blueprint for a visual story and as such everything in it needs to be visual and filmable so no internal writing about what a character feels or remembers – we should get that from how you externalize those feelings.

Break up action line chunks by story beat, audience focus or implied new camera angle so they stay below 5 lines each and keep the reader's eye flowing down the page.

Have you ever read a script where you thought "This writer gets it"? If so, what were the reasons why?

All the time! It's clear when a writer just doesn't know the rules versus a writer who knows the rules and breaks them creatively. These tend to be scripts with thoroughly developed characters, great pacing, and a satisfying emotional catharsis. They are scripts with a clear point of view and strong positive and negative stakes for the characters. Their message is the byproduct of a great story and not the sole reason for the story (i.e. the story isn't preachy).

How do you feel about screenwriting contests? Worth it or not?

It depends. If you do well in a big one, you can get noticed. The right ones can help you get representation or otherwise forward your project. For example, one of my clients just won the Nicholl. She will get lots of meetings off of that.

There are obviously a ton that are a waste of money but it can boost your confidence to get those laurels. There is a backside to that too. When I see scripts in competition with laurels on the title page (DO NOT DO THIS!), it's like they're painting a target on themselves saying "find reasons to tear this down" and, except in the rare occasion when it's a stellar script, we always can.

How can people find out more about you and the services you provide?

Visit us at www.pagecraftwriting.com. Our next round of script workshops starts in January, we offer one-on-one consulting services, and check out our Hearthside Salons podcast (on Podbean and iTunes) featuring conversations with writers, directors and other creatives.

Readers of this blog are more than familiar with my love/appreciation of pie. What's your favorite kind?

That's like asking me to pick a favorite sunset. I love anything fruit-related and made some killer loquat-ginger pies this spring. But I love pecan and pumpkin, so I'm happy it's that time of year. More pie!

Melody Jackson/Smart Girls Productions

Originally posted: Apr 6 2018

Melody Jackson, Ph.D., founder and CEO of Smart Girls Productions and Hollywood Business School, is a self-described "Marketing Person" and Entrepreneur. After working as a Marketing Person selling to the film industry for several years, she started Smart Girls Productions in 1992.

To learn more about Melody and the services provided by Smart Girls Productions, check out their screenwriting blog - www.smartg.com/screenwriters.

What's the last thing you read/watched that you thought was incredibly well-written?

That question is a little bit funky for me to answer and I'll tell you why. Years ago I took the famous/infamous Robert McKee screenwriting course, and there was one thing that really stuck with me. In that legendary, deep gruff voice with his big scary face belting from the stage, McKee shouted out: "I'm not doing this class to try to make you guys win Academy Awards.... I'm teaching this class to try to raise the overall quality of films that are out there." Something to that effect.

He talked about how, when he was a young boy, he would go watch every single film that came out in the theaters near him — even as a young kid, he went to see everything. All types of films. He just loved the medium of film.

The thing I learned from him is not to be so hung up on what is great writing, but to learn to enjoy film as a whole. Most scripts are not going to be great or really well-written. It's easy to critique and criticize most of them. But in that class, I learned to have a different perspective, and that makes a difference for me as a script analyst and for my clients.

Sure I can go deep into "analyzing" structure and character arcs and all kinds of stuff. But ultimately, it's a question first and foremost of "did this script cause me to have some kind of emotional experience? Regardless of anything else." Then, and only then, do I engage my left brain and start seeing how it could be made better. With better writing, you tend to appeal across a broader group of people.

How'd you get your start reading scripts?

Prior to starting my company Smart Girls Productions, I worked for a company that was involved with film distribution — both domestic and international — and I learned a fair amount about that. At one point, I just had to quit — no really good reason; they were great. But I just wanted to do a business on my own. That's when I started Smart Girls.

I was actually working on an acting career at that point and need to figure out how I was going to make money. Since I read scripts as an actress, I thought, "Hey, I could make money typing scripts." Yes, typing! I ran an ad in the Writer's Guild magazine and got a call right away. The truth is, I didn't even know how to type a script. I called an aspiring producer friend of mine who was also my mentor. And I asked him desperately, "How do I type a script?" He told me to get some book from Samuel French bookstore and I did. It took me forever to type those first two scripts. But after that, I typed a LOT of scripts…. we still do!

Then once I learned to type a script, I took lots of classes on screenwriting. Then I began writing my own scripts. Got hired to write a couple. I got a WGA agent. I went on to get my Ph.D. in mythological studies. And along the way, I added script analysis to my list of services and it turns out, I apparently have a knack for it. I ended up being rated one of the top 5 Script Consultants on three different occasions by Creative Screenwriting Magazine.

Your company's called Smart Girls Productions. What's the story behind the name, and what kind of work does the company do?

This one is short. When I started my company, I brainstormed a list of about 30 company names. I read it to my Mom, and she said, "Definitely Smart Girls." And so it was.

Told you it was short.

You have a PhD in Mythological Studies. Has that helped you in analyzing scripts?

For sure. Joseph Campbell, the father of bringing mythology into an understandable form, is the one who identified The Hero's Journey. That's the foundation of almost every great Western story. My studies in mythology looked at story from innumerable angles.... not just Campbell's but many others. So yes. It is in my DNA that it informs my analysis.

What are the components of a good script?

For me this is where the Hero's Journey meets Aristotle's POETICS. The Hero's Journey focuses more on the experience of the character and the inner transformation. The Poetics has more of an emphasis on plot. But if you work both angles, then you're going to have things that appeal to more audience members. That's the big picture.

If I had to say what those elements are, it would be something like... You need to have a character that has something he or she NEEDS to learn, some kind of lesson, some area of their life where they are misguided.

They then get pulled into some external plot in which they will be forced to confront that thing they have not learned. They will come face-to-face with it in the external plot. Their choice and how they handle it is the big lesson for them and for the audience. The biggest component for a good script for me is that the main character has some kind of transformation. That they are somehow a bigger, better or wiser character by the time the story ends.

What are some of the most common mistakes you see?

The most common big mistake I see is no solid theme developed in the story. You have to have some point to telling the story, otherwise it's a boring story about going to the store. Gotta have some point about human nature that is revealed in your story, or what's the point? That is the biggest mistake new writers make.

I would also venture to say it's also why more sophisticated moviegoers don't like straight-up action films. Too many times, the focus is not on any kind of transformation, but on other fun stuff like chase scenes and explosions and cool special effects. Nothing wrong with that, but it does nothing for the soul. The soul longs for transformation, and personal development. The theme is the highest articulation of that.

The most common mistake I see — actually I don't see it as a mistake, but more like the most underdeveloped aspect of scripts I read is theme. And I say it that way, because I find that most writers have some place of meaning they are writing from; they just haven't consciously identified what it is.

One of the non-writing necessities of screenwriting is the writer's ability to market themselves. Seeing as how that's one of your specialties, what are some key pieces of advice that writers should keep in mind?

You're not going to be successful overnight or next week. You're not going to sell your first script for a million dollars. Or even $250,000. The first person who reads your script is not going to fall in love with it and suddenly introduce you as this newly discovered gem that Hollywood has been waiting for.

Many screenwriters really have no idea how hard it is to get a deal and then get your movie made. It's a longshot. I'm not saying you should give up, but my best advice is to learn more about the BUSINESS side of the business. It's far more likely that a writer will get hired to rewrite a script if they're a great writer than it is that they will actually sell their film and have it be produced. Trying to convey this idea and educate writers on this is why I launched my Hollywood Business School at HollywoodBschool.com. My mission there is to help actors and writers better understand the business so they can have a much better chance at reaching their goals.

To boil it down to a few simple bits of advice: Keep learning as much as you can about the business. Get great at your craft. Market, market, market. Follow-up, follow-up, follow-up. Enjoy the pursuit. Be positive and be persistent. And don't quit your day job. BUT… do everything you can to help your career while you still have that job.

Part of your bio lists being the former emcee at the Hollywood Networking Breakfast. Could you provide a little more detail about the event and is it something screenwriters should consider attending?

My dear friend Sandra Lord is the Networking Guru of Hollywood. She was my manager for a period of time when I was acting. She started The Breakfast at that time, and she excelled at finding top level producers and agents to speak. For the nine years I emceed that and heard the speakers, I got a deep education in how Hollywood works and what execs want.

Sandra still hosts the breakfast several times a year. She also runs an event called "Let's Do Lunch" and the L.A. Film and Television Meetup. She is the first person that I recommend for every aspiring filmmaker, actor, set designer — anyone who wants to get into the business — go to her events as much as you can. You will definitely start making connections. And it's also not just for newbies. You'll find a lot of working industry people there as well.

What are the 3 most important rules every writer should know?

"Most" important? I tend to stay away from hyperbole because how can I really boil it down to MOST important? It's a great question that writers need to know, so it's not the question that's an issue — it's just my picky resistance to saying what is my most anything...Let me slightly modify and simply tell you what I think are some generally important rules. Here are the three I pick for now:

Learn story structure. Study screenwriting. If you haven't studied screenwriting, I guarantee you don't know how to do it well. 100% guaranteed.

Tap into your authenticity and write from there. In a very positive way, I think everyone has a great story to tell — of their own life even — if you find the right bits and pieces. Whatever it is that moves a screenwriter to spend weeks, months, and years on their screenplay, that tells me they have something important to say. This goes back to the theme I mentioned above. They may not have completely identified what their theme is — and why their story is important to them.

(But I will also guarantee this …. if they tap into their authenticity and why they are so moved by that story, that story will have a hundred times more impact — on them and their audience. If they get to their authenticity about it, there is deep fulfillment and satisfaction in writing a story like that. Then your passion makes it much easier for others to see its greatness.)

Don't take anything you hear from a producer or agent at face value. You have to know how to read between the lines.

What story tropes are you just tired of seeing?

It's less a story trope that I'm tired of because they can be told in different ways. What I find hard to watch or read is when the writer or filmmakers have not tapped into their unique vision — again I would call it lacking authenticity — but then … I don't want THAT to come across as a TROPE! If I had to say it another way, it's when people are not digging deep enough into their soul to get to their authentic, unique perspective.

You could see the same story ten different times and if the filmmakers or screenwriter truly tapped into their own unique take deep within, it could still be interesting. It's like when a great song is recorded by many different artists. Whether it's "Over the Rainbow," "Amazing Grace," "Yesterday," "Can't Help Falling In Love" or "To Love Somebody," when a great singer does their unique rendition, we can hear it over and over and still be moved by it. The same with a story or a story beat. The problem lies in the lack of tapping into the truth of the individual writer.

Readers of this blog are more than familiar with my love/appreciation of pie. What's your favorite kind?

Gotta be pumpkin! I need to find a good source for pumpkin pie here in Los Angeles. Got one?

Craig Kellem & Judy Hammett/Hollywoodscript.com

Originally posted: Mar 8 2019

Hollywoodscript.com LLC was founded over a decade ago by former Universal and Fox development executive Craig Kellem, who was soon joined by business partner Judy Hammett (M.A. English/Creative Writing). This family-based, boutique script consultation service is internationally known, serving writers from every corner of the world.

I had the pleasure of talking with Judy about their new book GET IT ON THE PAGE: TOP SCRIPT CONSULTANTS SHOW YOU HOW.

What's the last thing you read or watched that you thought was incredibly well written?

Without a doubt, HBO's most recent season (#3) of TRUE DETECTIVE. It is truly impressive every week. The writer has an incredible command of dialogue and the structure employed is beautiful. The writer has interwoven various timelines in a very clever and elegant way, wherein the plotline is consistently advanced, yet at the same time, the existential themes being explored are made exceptionally dramatic and emotionally charged as a result.

How'd you get your start in the industry?

We are father and daughter and come from a family that made their living in TV and music, so we both got our first breaks through family/friends. Craig started out as an assistant at a talent agency and worked hard up the ranks to become a talent agent himself. He eventually became a development executive at Fox and Universal, and in time a TV Producer as well. I started as a researcher on a TV series, then did freelance work providing studio coverage on scripts & books while in graduate school for English/Creative Writing. Eventually, Craig founded our company, Hollywoodscript.com LLC and I joined him soon thereafter. We've worked together for more than fifteen years.

Were you always writers, or was it something you eventually discovered you had a knack for?

We've always tended to "think" like writers, and have loved writing just for the sheer pleasure it provides! But neither of us chose to "become" professional writers, or pursue careers as such. We both love working with writers, supporting their craft and analyzing content. This has been our true vocation. We wrote our book together from the standpoint of wanting to reach out to writers everywhere and share what we have learned after almost two decades of consulting with writers the world over. I provide writing services/ghostwriting on occasion, but consulting is my main work.

What inspired you to write your book GET IT ON THE PAGE: TOP SCRIPT CONSULTANTS SHOW YOU HOW?

Over the years we had clients comment that we should write a book, stating that our general feedback and approach was constructive, inspired and very helpful. So a few years ago, we decided it was time to give the book idea a green light and started putting the chapters together – with the sole purpose of sharing observations and approaches to writing, which have proven the most helpful to writers we've worked with to date.

With so many screenwriting books out there, what is it about yours that makes it especially unique?

We hope to offer something which is more intuitive, less "left brain" – a book that invites the writer to stay close to their own experiences, their own strong feelings and their own instincts so that the storyteller inside of them can more easily come to the fore.

Follow-up: having read a lot of screenwriting books, I found this one to be very different in that it's not so much about "how to", but more of a "here's something to consider as you work on your story/script". Was that your initial intent, or did it gradually develop that way?

Many thanks for your feedback! Yes, that is a wonderful way to describe it. We didn't set out to compete with the screenwriting greats who've written comprehensive "how-tos" beautifully and exhaustively. Instead, we wanted to contribute to the conversation from the hands-on perspective of our day-to-day work with a very diverse range of writers – some of whom have studied the gamut of how-to books, yet continue to struggle with actually realizing their own visions on the page. We wanted to offer a book that helps writers get closer to "hearing" their "own voice" so to speak – to accessing the vivid, original stories and characters that live inside of them.

One of the chapters that really resonated with me was the one about the practice you call "sandboxing". Could you explain what you mean by that, and how it could benefit a writer?

Inspiration, ideas and the desire to write often come out of writers having creative shards and glimmers that have emerged from their minds. They get an idea for a scene late at night and jot it down on scrap paper. They encounter some person they think would make a great character type and make a note of it on a napkin. They hear an anecdote that suggests a story and scribble it on an envelope.

All these pieces of creative inspiration are wonderful fuel for writing a screenplay, but a few glimmers and shards aren't enough to justify starting at page one of a one-hundred-plus-page three-act film. Yet zealous writers will often do just that. They plow forward on the faint fumes of too few ideas and assure themselves the rest will come as they write. This approach rarely makes the cut, for the writer hasn't given enough time and thought to what it is they are actually writing.

Rather than starting a screenplay prematurely, we therefore recommend "sandboxing," which is a simple method wherein the writer slows down in order to create a much bigger arsenal of ideas from which to choose. Each day they jot down additional possibilities for scenes, character angles, key plot lines etc. – adding to their original seeds of inspiration. It thoroughly preps the writer to eventually sit down to page one of their new script armed with a truckload of ideas from which to write.

What do you consider the components of a good solid script?

A clear, strong story is key. Characters who are relatable and believable. A hero with whom the audience can empathize and who breaks into a serious sweat as much as possible. Dialogue that rings true. Lots of suspense, urgency, and conflict that keep the audience riveted and the pacing clipped.

What are some key rules/guidelines every writer should know?

Writing IS rewriting, even when you're a pro, so best to embrace this notion and learn to enjoy the process of writing, revising and polishing your script before declaring it "done".

Getting a script sold, or made, doesn't happen on any predictable timeline. Just keep writing and derive your pleasure from the creative process, rather than focusing on it as a means to an end.

If you are cloudy about any part of your script, stop and take the time to fully explore that cloudiness, addressing it head-on. Don't try to finesse it, or gloss over it, or avoid it in order to deal with the parts of the script that are clearer to you. Otherwise, your audience may get stuck in those foggy sequences and then start detaching from your content as a whole.

Never lose sight of the fact that a film is a visual art form. As you write, always ask yourself if there's a way to dramatize the story development through images, cinematic sequences and visual cues first and foremost.

What are some of the most common screenwriting mistakes you see?

Writers who tend to overwrite and hence interfere with needed momentum. Setting a strong, galloping pace is essential.

Scripts that are confusing because the writer hasn't maintained consistent continuity in the plot line or in terms of the character trajectories.

Scenes that don't build the story or move narratives in the film forward.

How can people find out more about you and the services you provide?
We can be found at hollywoodscript.com and are on Twitter (@hollywoodscrip1), Facebook, and Linked In – Craig and Judy. And of course, check out our book GET IT ON THE PAGE: TOP SCRIPT CONSULTANTS SHOW YOU HOW.

Readers of this blog are more than familiar with my love/appreciation of pie. What's your favorite kind?

HA! I'll take pie over cake any day – especially coconut, chocolate, vanilla or banana cream. Craig likes ice cream too much to think about any other type of dessert.

Jeff Kitchen

Originally posted: Apr 10 2020

Jeff Kitchen was classically trained in playwriting technique, specializing in the work of the groundbreaking Broadway script doctor William Thompson Price.

Jeff worked as a dramaturg in the New York theater, Playwrights Preview Productions (now Urban Stages) and taught playwriting on Broadway at the Negro Ensemble Company. He then started teaching screenwriting and has taught for over twenty years in small high-intensity hands-on groups.

He teaches the craft of the dramatist, advanced structural technique, the core of dramatic action, script analysis, and plot construction. Jeff is a sought-after script doctor, plot construction specialist, and rewrite consultant.

He has taught his techniques to development execs from all the major Hollywood studios and they consistently say that he teaches the most advanced development tools in the industry.

One of his students, Ted Melfi, was recently nominated for Best Picture and Best Adapted Screenplay Academy Awards for his film about the black women mathematicians at NASA, HIDDEN FIGURES.

Jeff is the author of the book, WRITING A GREAT MOVIE: KEY TOOLS FOR SUCCESSFUL SCREENWRITING. Jeff is now doing high-intensity training programs for professional scriptwriters as well as script consulting.

What's the last thing you read or watched that you thought was incredibly well-written?

NARCOS: MEXICO on Netflix. It was so gripping, so watchable. Hard to believe it was true. I kept telling my wife how great it is, and said to her several times I thought it was better than THE GODFATHER. They move through so much story in just two seasons, with so much intensity and depth, great casting and acting, great writing, and so much material to weave together. The corruption makes your blood boil; the loss, the genius, the brutality, the nobility, the adventure, the chess game, the betrayal, the power and murder and love and ambition, and the pure history—there's so much going on and it's so compelling.

How'd you get your start in the industry?

I was mostly self-taught. A friend who was a playwright taught me the basics of Aristotle and gave me two old obscure books on playwriting to read. They were quite fascinating and very difficult, but I spent three years studying them intensely. The guy who wrote one of them, William Thompson Price, was a pioneering Broadway script doctor for top producers pre-1920 and he founded the first school of playwriting ever in the history of the world. Twenty-four of his twenty-eight students had hits on Broadway.

Price created several seriously groundbreaking tools for the dramatist and I emerged with a mastery of what he created, then improved on them and taught these tools nonstop for twenty years. People kept saying they'd never seen anything like what I taught and said they worked better than anything they'd seen. I trained development execs at all the major Hollywood studios and they consistently said I taught the most advanced development tools in the industry. So I found these old tools and ideas for tools, and studied them like crazy, then synthesized them into their current form. I taught and consulted with them for years, and got deeply experienced with them from working hands-on with them on thousands of students' works in progress.

What do you consider the components of a good script?

The short answer to that question is my 352-page book, WRITING A GREAT MOVIE. Of course I can say something in a paragraph or two, but a proper answer can go deep and wide and long. A great premise, first of all, because if your raw idea sucks, then no amount of structure or character or storytelling elbow grease will get that clunker up in the air as a commercially viable project. In the industry, it's called Polishing a Turd. I always say well-structured crap is still crap. So start with a great idea.

Also crucial is a good strong Dilemma of Magnitude for the protagonist, but it's not easy in such a brief format to properly communicate how to make that one dilemma occupy the full proportion of the script, build to a Crisis, force Decision and Action in the face of crisis, and then conclude with the protagonist's active Resolution of the dilemma. The way in which the protagonist resolves the dilemma expresses the Theme, and it's crucial to have a solid sense of theme as you build your story.

You need distinct characters who are deep and complex and colorful in various ways, and who are deeply flawed, contradictory and universal.

You need to attack as a storyteller, so you're not making safe, cliché, or stock choices. Your script must be actable and it has to be stageworthy. The action of the story must move ahead aggressively, with nothing unnecessary bogging it down. It needs good cause and effect, escalating conflict, structural unity, dramatic action, and so much more. But mostly, it has to hit the audience where they live. If it doesn't connect to the audience, then it's not compelling.

What are some of the most common screenwriting mistakes you see?

Weak ideas, lack of imagination, lack of attack, poor execution, poor structure, lazy storytelling, stale characters, lack of depth, lack of color, overwriting, over-describing, overbearing, too much exposition, attempting to dictate an emotional response rather than earning it, lack of empathy for the main characters, underpowered ending, doesn't pass the So What? test, crappy dialog, boring, derivative, packs no punch, uneven tone, peters out, holes in the story's logic, lack of conflict, no clear goal for the protagonist, stupid, a simple plot vs a complex plot, episodic, formulaic, wooden characters, preachy, predictable, miserable writing skills, lack of follow-through, writing not cinematic, story not commercially viable, no sense of vision, no entertainment value, flat dramatically, lack of magnitude.

Just to name a few.

What story tropes are you just tired of seeing?

I'm not sure how many more serial killers I want to read about, or how many more procedurals, or special forces dudes, or nuclear annihilation. They can all get tiresome, but it obviously has to do with the execution, because each of them can kick serious ass when done well. But I think that things like a serial killer can be just a cardboard prop or a vastly overused excuse to write something brutal and adventurous for people who can't or won't do the work to go deeper and find a freakier way to mess with people's heads.

Watch a movie like BAD BOY BUBBY or BAD LIEUTENANT with Harvey Keitel to see something fresh and wacko. People sleepwalk through the writing process sometimes, and it's tedious because so many people are out there writing the same warmed-over tales. There's probably room for a story about a serial killer who kills writers who are writing about serial killers.

What are some key rules/guidelines every writer should know?

Shake things up. You're a writer. Do something to me, mess with my head, defy my expectations, violate my sense of how a story should go. Tell a story that really tweaks me, that seriously makes me care, that grabs me by the throat and makes me notice. Make me fall in love, or go through something unimaginable, or face death, or embrace life—but do it full tilt and do it well. I don't need the same old tired stories coming at me all day long. I'm looking for adventure, depth, love, heartbreak, power, in any genre.

Make the overall structure for your story work first. If it does not, then the details do not matter. A beautifully written scene in a script that doesn't work is meaningless. It's like having an ornately finished room in a house that's falling down. Learn to work from the general to the particular. Make the overall story work, then make each act work, then each sequence, and then each scene. You gradually develop and dramatize your work as you build it.

Learn to separate the Necessary from the Unnecessary. The work of the amateur is characterized by the Unnecessary. Dialogue and description are overwritten, scenes may not be needed, whole sequences may only be dead weight, sometimes an entire act can end up being unnecessary, and in fact your entire script may be unnecessary. Which may sound funny, but it's not. The Unnecessary kills scripts. Most scripts are unreadable—and that means 98% of them—UN-READ-ABLE. Atrocious. And in many instances, the Unnecessary plays a major part in how unreadable it is. Clean, crisp cause and effect separates the Necessary from the Unnecessary, and moves the action of the story ahead crisply and cleanly.

Master the craft of the dramatist. Dramatic writing is generally considered the most elusive of all the literary disciplines. It's tricky, it's slippery, it's hard to pin down, hard to predict, and hard to diagnose or cure. But the more craft you've got, the more mastery you have in addressing every type of problem. People forget that scriptwriting is a performance medium—intended to be acted out in front of an audience in such a way that it's gripping. So take the time to really learn your craft, to master it.

Because almost doesn't count, and people don't want to read scripts that could have been good but the writer didn't have the chops to make it work.

Take the time to build or discover deep, complex, dynamic, unpredictable, flawed, dimensional characters. Explore the Enneagram (EnneagramInstitute.com is a great resource) for each of your main characters because it's such a remarkably powerful resource. A mixture of ancient wisdom about human nature and cutting-edge psychology, it purports that there are nine basic personality types, and each of these types has a healthy aspect, an average aspect, and unhealthy aspects. This helps you go deep and complex, to develop substantial flaws, hidden strengths, the mechanics of failure, a path to greatness, and complex, sophisticated human emotional reality.

What was the inspiration/motivation for your book WRITING A GREAT MOVIE?

I wanted to get down on paper the know-how I'd accrued from teaching non-stop for eighteen years while it was still white hot. I had always taught small hands-on classes, maximum six people, and each person had to bring a script idea with them to develop so I could really get them using the tools. This helped them not only learn how to use the tools, but their scripts improved so much in the process that word of mouth on my classes was through the roof. I never taught large groups because the material was too complex. I knew that if I just talked at people about sophisticated techniques without showing them how to really use the tools that it would be mostly useless, because they couldn't go home and use it to build their own script.

But when they started doing a big Screenwriter's Expo in LA, they dragged me into teaching 150 people at a time. And there were riots outside my classroom of people trying to get in, so I realized that with this many people having heard about my training, it was time to write my book. So I cranked one out and self-published it by the next year's Expo and sold a lot of them. I shopped that version and it got me a lit agent in New York who got me a publishing deal at Watson Guptill where two phenomenal editors helped bring out the best in my writing.

There are a lot of screenwriting books out there. What about this one makes it unique?

Not only are the tools unique, unusual and powerful, but I worked hard to emulate the hands-on aspect of my small classes in which I worked with each participant on their script as I explained the tools. So I explain, illustrate, and demonstrate each of seven tools in the first half of the book, and then I build a real script from scratch in the second half of the book, using all the tools. I start with a one-line idea and build the whole script, demonstrating the full use of the tools as I utilize them to create, develop, structure and write it.

Because I was rewriting the self-published edition, my editor wanted to clean up the second half of the book. I argued, saying that it had to remain unvarnished because the process of using these tools to create from scratch is necessarily messy. I needed it to remain fumbling and exploratory and rough, because cobbling a story together and dramatizing it is like feeling your way along in the dark. And I wanted to show them the raw reality, not the cleaned-up varnished version.

In the introduction to part two, I say that the first half of the book is as different from the second half as training in medical school is from working in an Emergency Room, or as studying a bear in the zoo is from wrestling one in the wilderness. I jump from tool to tool bootstrapping the story into existence, using Dilemma, the Enneagram, the 36 Dramatic Situations, Crisis, Theme, Research and Brainstorming all at the same time. And then I put the story through two structural tools, the Central Proposition and Sequence, Proposition, Plot, which help dramatize the narrative, strip out everything that's unnecessary to the forward action of the story, and create consistent, coherent, compelling Dramatic Action.

I build the whole script with my readers looking over my shoulder, and I think it did a good job of showing the tools in action in order to give the reader genuine know-how and experience in utilizing the tools.

How do you feel about screenwriting contests? Worth it or not?

The top five or ten are definitely worth it and have launched many careers. I myself wouldn't bother with many others, but it totally depends on what you're up to as a writer. If you just want to put your stuff out there to see what people think of it, then you can use it as a learning opportunity. But you can also just hire somebody to give you notes on your script and that might give you more specific feedback. But there are books and websites that can help you sort the contests for value, and people who know everything about them, and they're definitely worth taking a look at as part of a career strategy.

How can people find out more about you and the services you provide?

My website is BuildYourScript.com and I can be contacted through there or directly at jeffkitchen88@gmail.com. I offer a free class on Reverse Cause and Effect at my site. This is a powerful class that shows how to take a story you've roughed out and work backward from the ending, chaining backward from each effect to its cause. This enables you to stitch together the main building blocks of your story, and then to gradually flesh out the details as they become necessary. I demonstrate the process in action by working on a real script.

There's also a paid class on a remarkably powerful plot construction tool called Sequence, Proposition, Plot which is a groundbreaking way to structure and develop your script, working from the big picture down to the details. I do consults on scripts as well as private classes on technique. One of the coolest things I do is to help people build their script from scratch, or to work with them rebuilding it once they've gotten a script up and running.

I'm about to roll a high-intensity training program for scriptwriters that I'm really excited about. It's an online immersion program in which I train apprentices for a year as we work together building multiple scripts. We'll work two hours a day, plus one hour of homework, five days a week. In what's called a Community of Practice, I communicate know-how through using the tools to build real scripts on the spot, and I also have students do extensive drills and rigorous exercises, handling the tools, practicing them over and over, and learning to think in that language until it all becomes second nature.

This type of learning process is called Cognitive Apprenticeship, in which writers work hand-in-glove with me to learn how to think like me. I communicate both explicit knowledge and the more ambiguous but crucial tacit knowledge, that feel for things which are indispensable for full expertise. This will be a high-intensity program, similar to a trade school, followed by a year in which I work with these highly-trained writers on building their own scripts. They will emerge as trained dramatists with key skills and experience, who can forge a career as working writers.

Readers of this blog are more than familiar with my love/appreciation of pie. What's your favorite kind?

It's hard to pick, but right now I'd have to go with cherry.

Jon Kohan

Originally posted: Nov 15 2019

Jon Kohan is a script consultant and award-winning screenwriter from Johnstown, PA, who's worked in both film and television. His horror/comedy short FAMILY GAME NIGHT earned him a Best Screenwriter nomination from the Shock Stock film festival (along with winning for Best Actor), and his holiday comedy DEER GRANDMA won Best Comedy at the Show Low Film Festival.

His project PURPLE GANG is a pilot based on the Purple Gang who operated out of Detroit predominantly in the 1920's and 1930's, with over 300 members during their tenure. The series will be inspired by real life characters and events but will not be a non-fiction story.

His comedy/crime short SPILLED PAINT picked up several Best Short and Best Cast awards on the festival circuit, and is available on YouTube.

What's the last thing you read or watched that you thought was incredibly well-written?

MINDHUNTER, season two, on Netflix. The first season was great, and the second was just as good. I love the show for all the tension-filled scenes that can last ten-plus minutes, and usually just between two or three characters. The writers of that show are super-talented, and I look forward to being able to read and study the scripts to see how to improve my own writing.

How'd you get your start in the industry?

The lead-up is a pretty long story- working different writing jobs as I gained more experience and building a resume of work – but I'll talk about how I landed my first real gig.

I was doing freelance writing work on a site called Fiverr.com. I still use the site from time-to-time. On my page, at the time, I offered joke writing and screenwriting, but only for shorts.

I had a customer hire me for a short story idea they had. I worked on it for about a week and sent it back to them. A couple weeks go by and that customer comes back and says they have an idea for a family film that could even be a television show but needs someone they feel has the talent and skill to write a pilot; maybe even possibly a whole first season.

I jumped at the chance to work on that script, and in fact did write the pilot and the entire first season (10 episodes). About a year after I wrote the pilot, the customer reached out to me again to let me know that the project was going into production. That customer's name was Alvin Williams. Since working on that pilot, titled ERNIE AND CERBIE (currently streaming on Amazon Prime), we've teamed up on multiple projects and he's become one of my main collaborators in the industry.

Is recognizing good writing something you think can be taught or learned?

Anyone can probably be taught or learn how to recognize good writing, but something you can't teach is how to tell a good story. Not everyone can do that. Just because you can write doesn't mean you can tell a story in the film or television format.

The rules/guidelines of writing a script is what I think makes screenwriting harder
than with other forms of writing. And not everyone can tell an entertaining story. Knowing and understanding what good writing is and looks like makes the viewer smarter, which allows for smarter movies. With a smarter audience, there'll be a need for more originality – fresh perspectives, which will hopefully open the door to a more diverse and new pool of writers.

What do you consider the components of a good script?

This could be a very long list, but it all trickles down to one major core component: characters.

Not enough big Hollywood movies take the time to craft a film around strong characters, and instead try to build a film around a plot, or worse, action sequences, tone, look, etc. What do THE DARK KNIGHT and JOKER have in common other than the obvious that both are Batman films? They're two of DC's best films, and both focus more on character than all the craziness around them.

If you have characters we care about, can relate to, or at least understand where they're coming from, and put them into conflicts that help our characters grow and become something more, you have a winner on your hands.

Even if your film is more about the concept (INDEPENDENCE DAY, GODZILLA), if you take the time to do the proper character work, you can throw a great one-two punch, something most Hollywood films seem to be lacking nowadays.

What are some of the most common screenwriting mistakes you see?

Formatting issues. No question. Not everyone uses screenwriting software, which is weird to me. If you're not just writing a script as a hobby, you should invest in the proper industry tools.
I see formatting issues all the time, and those can easily be fixed, and quickly learned.

One of the most common things to see is a script not written like one. So many writers write action lines like they're writing a novel. Telling us what the character is thinking, why they're doing something a certain way, what's going to happen later without us ever seeing it later.

I urge to my clients how "Show, Don't Tell" is a huge rule they should always be repeating to themselves. How do you present information in a film or TV show? Either through images or dialogue. If we don't see it or hear it, we don't know it. When I have a writer I'm working with go back and look at their script again – with that guideline in mind – they'll see just how much information is in their script that they are telling the reader, but not showing them.

What story tropes are you just tired of seeing?

I don't know which I hate more: "You lied to me?" or "There is a prophecy...." The first is something you hear more in comedies. The second you always hear in fantasy, adventure, action, etc. If I'm watching a romcom, I KNOW the end of the second act will have "You lied to me?" as dialogue – usually from the female lead.

For most summer blockbusters, fantasy films, the trailer is probably going to have some version of the "There is a prophecy..." line, and the entire setup will be this typical paint-by-numbers hero's journey story.

What are some key rules/guidelines every writer should know?

Show, Don't Tell. (see my response a few questions back)

Formatting – I know just looking at the first page if the read is going to be enjoyable or if it's going to feel like I'm doing homework. That all stems from the format of the script. If I can glance and see issues, then I know there's going to be issues with the characters, story, arcs, and so on. Even if you can tell a story, or write good characters, and have something actually happen in your script, at least make the script look like a script. This sets the tone for your reader and lets them know you know what you're doing. As a writer, your goal is to get someone to read your script.

A horribly-formatted script is an easy excuse for someone not to take the time to read your script. Don't give them that choice.

DON'T WRITE CAMERA DIRECTIONS! – This is something a lot of first-time writers do in their scripts. I was no different. Learning how to write your action lines properly and how to influence the director in shooting a scene a certain way by the way it's written not only makes your script stand out amongst the others but it'll make you a better writer as a whole. I know it has for me, or at least think it has.

Have you ever read a spec script that was an absolute, without-a-doubt "recommend"? If so, what were the reasons why?

I've read scripts from screenwriting friends of mine that have really impressed me. Some of them are super talented, award-winning writers who are going to be names we recognize one day.

As far as reading a spec script that was sent to me to review and give detailed notes on, I haven't read a script yet I'd stamp "recommend". Some have come close, but unless you're lucky and extremely talented, it's not going to be your first script that you do something with.
The more scripts you write, the better you'll be. My first script is god-awful compared to my tenth script, and my tenth script is amateurish compared to the latest draft of a script I recently finished.

What would a script need to get a "recommend" from me? As I keep saying, strong characters. Throw in a joke once in a while.

Make me want to keep turning the pages. One of the worst things to see is a massive block of action or dialogue, and know the whole script is going to be that way. The more white on the page, the better.

A script could be for the greatest movie ever made, but if it's a difficult chore to read and takes hours – or even days – to complete, I probably won't see it as a recommended script.

How do you feel about screenwriting contests? Worth it or not?

Worth it – for sure. Screenwriting contests are great to try and win some awards, network with other screenwriters and filmmakers, and get yourself exposure.

With all that being said, if you place in or even win one of the top contests, that's going to open a lot more doors for you than winning a much smaller contest.

I don't agree that you must enter contests to be able to get a film produced. I've only recently started entering contests and already have several produced projects under my belt, with and more in development.

How can people find out more about you and the services you provide?

My website, www.screenwriterjon.com, my Patreon www.patreon.com/screenwriterjon, and my Fiverr www.fiverr.com/jonkohan. You can also check out all of my projects on my IMDB page.

On my Patreon, I offer screenwriting and script feedback services through two different subscription tiers. I've already had two filmmakers subscribe to have me write their feature films, so that's been really exciting.

Readers of this blog are more than familiar with my love/appreciation of pie. What's your favorite kind?

I bet you haven't heard this one before – Oreo. Store bought or homemade. Either works for me. I have a huge sweet tooth. This may sound like a little kid answer, but it's the truth.

Victoria Lucas/Lucas Script Consulting

Originally posted: Mar 20 2020

Victoria Lucas has more than 20 years of experience as a development and production executive at both major studios and independent film companies. She began her career with Ron Howard at Imagine Entertainment, working on films including CLEAN AND SOBER, BACKDRAFT, and FAR AND AWAY.

She later joined with Academy Award-nominated producer Rudy Cohen to develop and produce the acclaimed coming-of-age film THE ISLAND ON BIRD STREET (winner of three Emmys and two awards at the Berlin International Film Festival). As Director of Development, Production Executive and Associate Producer at Signature Entertainment and April Productions, Lucas helped develop projects as diverse as THE BLACK DAHLIA, THE I INSIDE, and THE BODY.

Lucas currently works as an independent producer and runs a professional screenplay development service for producers, production companies and screenwriters. She is also the on-air host for Arizona Public Media's Saturday night feature film program, HOLLYWOOD AT HOME, providing historical background and an insider's look at the making of classic films.

What was the last thing you read/watched that you considered to be extremely well-written?

PARASITE. I was highly impressed by that script, especially the way the writers managed to switch plot directions – and even genres – so seamlessly. In fact, I feel that films, television and streaming shows are in something of a "Golden Age of Writing" at the moment. For instance, look at two other recent films: JOKER and KNIVES OUT. I'm in awe of how Todd Phillips and Scott Silver managed to make us sympathetic to the characters in JOKER (helped, of course, by Joaquin Phoenix's amazing performance). And Rian Johnson did a masterful job of updating and reinvigorating old Agatha Christie tropes in KNIVES OUT.

How'd you get your start in the industry?

To be honest, it all started at birth. My mother, father and two grandparents were in the industry, with both my dad and grandma being successful screenwriters. I grew up in a house where writing was an everyday job, and it was taken very, very seriously. Unfortunately, their talent didn't rub off on me, but I discovered through reading my dad's work – and hearing about the process it went through before reaching the screen – that my real interest lay in working with writers to develop their scripts. From there, my career began as a reader, followed a pretty straightforward trajectory: producer's assistant, story editor, creative executive, director of development, then into production.

Is recognizing good writing something you think can be taught or learned?

I learned to recognize good writing through years of reading and discussion at home growing up. But if you're asking whether good writing can itself be taught or learned, the answer is "Yes, I think it can."

Screenwriting is both an art and a craft. You might be born with a talent for telling stories, but that's only half the equation. Putting those stories onto paper in a way that will appeal to producers and audiences is the other half, and that's the hard part. You need to hone your technique; or, put another way, to "develop your writing muscles." Screenwriting classes, writers' groups, how-to-books, blogs and podcasts – all can help. One of my favorite podcasts is SCRIPTNOTES with John August and Craig Mazin.

But the bottom line is this: You have to sit in your chair and write. And write. And write some more. No matter how naturally talented you are, you must practice your craft. It's no different than becoming a master painter, concert musician or sports star. The more you do it, the better you become.

In the end, though, every writer is different; each with their own technique. Some like to outline their story so they know exactly how it will unfold before they begin to write. Others prefer to let the characters "tell" them what's going to happen. Some are naturals at structure; others write great dialogue. The challenge for a writer is to identify the elements of screenwriting that don't come naturally, then work hard to improve them.

What do you consider the components of a good script?

A script is the blueprint for a movie, and the drawing begins with the concept. A great premise is like having an engine that drives the plot and the characters. If it is strong enough, it acts as the spine of the movie so that the structural elements – a compelling story, memorable characters, exciting action and all the rest – will fit together and support each other to produce a successful on-screen result. It's not enough to create a literary masterpiece that's envisioned entirely in the reader's head; if the script lacks cinematic elements, it's unlikely to get produced.

What are some of the most common screenwriting mistakes you see?

I know writers are tired of hearing about it – and many will simply ignore the advice — but the way you present your screenplay is more important than you think. That means formatting to industry standards and doing more than a cursory spellcheck. Now, I can guarantee you that no producer ever passed on a great script because of a few spelling mistakes, but the script had to get to her in the first place. You need to realize that the first person to read your screenplay is likely to be a junior development person, an assistant or even an intern. Most of those people have a dozen or more scripts to plow through every week before the company staff meeting. If your script looks unprofessional with too many formatting errors, it's far too easy for it to be put down.

A common mistake among emerging screenwriters is to overload a script with plot. Cramming in too many plots and subplots doesn't allow you to develop the characters within the story. So, while a lot might happen, it's hard to care about the people involved. Conversely, you don't want a story where nothing seems to happen or change. Films are about conflict and drama. Always think, "What's at stake?"

Passive lead characters are problematic. Hamlet may be indecisive but he's not passive. In a similar vein, try not to fall onto the trap of creating supporting roles that are vivid and cinematic, while your hero is bland and uninteresting.

And please, please avoid using dialogue as exposition. I cringe every time a line starts with, "As you know…" or "Do you remember when we…?" That's designed to give information or back story to the audience; it's not something real characters would say to one another. Incidentally, when I was a young development exec, my friends and I used to compete for the best (read: worst) lines of expository dialogue. I won with "Tell me again why we're going to Grandma's."

What story tropes are you just tired of seeing?

It's disheartening to me to find spec scripts that are pale imitations of the hot new movie or television show that just came out. Even experienced writers often forget that by the time a film is released or debuts as a series, the studio pipeline is already filled with similar projects. Rather than chase after what seems to be commercial at the time, write a great story that you feel passionate about – one that may change the direction of what's commercial, just as George Lucas (no relation) did with sci-fi in 1977.

What are some key rules/guidelines every writer should know?

Read scripts. As many as you can. Then read some more. You can easily find Academy Award winning screenplays online, but don't limit yourself to the greats. Mediocre or bad scripts can teach you a great deal… even if it's "what not to do." One often-overlooked element in screenwriting is structure. The classic three-act structure is the norm in a majority of American films, but there's nothing magical about it: more and more scripts are written in five acts.

However, every script needs a structure just as a building needs a foundation.

There's a truism in films: writing is rewriting. You may feel that you've finished your work after you write Fade Out. But really, you're just beginning. Most of the films I was involved with averaged 9 drafts before production started – and that's on top of however many drafts the writer did before submitting the script! Learn how to take notes. Films are collaborative and, unless you write, produce, direct, finance and star in your movie, you will be getting notes. You might not agree with or accept all of them, but do be open to outside ideas that can help your script. Writers groan (often quite rightly) about "development hell," but the reality is that most scripts can be improved.

Have you ever read a spec script that was an absolute, without-a-doubt "recommend"? If so, what were the reasons why?

I've probably read over ten thousand scripts in my career, and I remember giving four straight-up recommends. That doesn't mean I haven't read dozens or even hundreds of superb scripts, but a development executive's job is to find projects for her production company. If the company I work with produces mainly action films and I read an outstanding character drama... well, no matter how brilliant it is, it's not a script I can recommend to the producers. Mind you, if the script is that good, I'll for sure find out more about that writer and, at the very least, see if they might have something else I can take to the producer.

How do you feel about screenwriting contests? Worth it or not?

Absolutely worth it! But be selective. There are too many contests out there that only want to take your entry fee. Do your homework and find the reputable ones. Nothing about the film business is easy, but placing well in the most prestigious contests can be a great calling card for a new writer, helping you get representation or even producers asking to read your screenplay.

Some of the top contests use industry professionals as judges, especially for the finalists. This can be a big plus: If they read your script and find it's a good fit for their company or agency, you'll be hearing from them after the contest even if you don't win.

How can people find out more about you and the services you provide?

My company is Lucas Script Consulting (www.lucasscript.com). All the information you need is on the website, including a link to contact me.

Readers of this blog are more than familiar with my love/appreciation of pie. What's your favorite kind?

Cherry. Ideally made with tart (sometimes called sour) cherries. Bliss!

Terry McFadden/Story Builders

Originally posted: Apr 24 2020

Terry McFadden came up through the ranks as a playwright having been produced throughout the United States, the UK and Australia and winning several awards. From there he worked as a script consultant for ARD Television, Radio and Films and Eternity Pictures before starting off on his own. He has had the good fortune of giving studio notes to producers on scripts that got made such as THE GOOD GIRL, CONFESSIONS OF A DANGEROUS MIND and THE TRUTH ABOUT CHARLIE.

As the founder of Story Builders Script Doctor & Writing Services, he has covered, analyzed, given notes and consulted on hundreds of screenplays, TV pilots and story ideas and is dedicated to helping writers find and hone their own unique voice.

What's the last thing you read or watched you thought was incredibly well-written?

JOKER. Without question. The absolute best script of 2019. From the very first page I loved the writing. Now, a lot of it is because I so identify with the charm and depth, the way it was done, the thematic and stylistic elements hit me right off. Not only was the lead character great and unique but he starts out as a very human but weird guy who has issues—issues that are clearly foreshadowed and then evolved. The story makes clear and piece by piece layers in not only his mental and delusional maladjustments but the idea that the way things turn out, as a result of his upbringing and belief systems and how he sees himself and world, is the only way it can end. This is developed wonderfully.

Screenwriters are taught to look at story, the characters and their arc, the twists, the spins, the reversals, the progressive development and surprises; a solid and rising structure with the catalyst plot points, midpoint, and the rest. All of that was there in JOKER but what kept me turning pages was the way it all weaved back in—supporting and commenting on what is already going on adding dimension. A real fresh slant on how he becomes not only his own hero but also the hero of those in need of such a person. The metaphors, the allegories, the songs, the running symbolic commentary—all snaking back and endorsing what is going on or will be, was both unpredictable, cool, necessary yet not seen coming in that way. Very well done.

How'd you get your start in the industry?

I started as a musician. Eight years old, I'm taking guitar lessons and my Dad tosses me onstage with "Tommy Schaefer's Country/Polka Band at Jim Thorpe Memorial Park". Music is a big part of everything I do. Writing is music. I came to formal writing at Penn State, penning funny essays about people and teachers. But it took off in Los Angeles in 1993 or so, when I began to write short scenes and monologues for the theatre. I became a member of Actors Art Theatre in Hollywood and remained there for four and a half years—this is where I really developed my style of writing.

Writing scenes progressed to ten-minute plays, short plays and one-acts. The director and founder of the theatre was a real mentor to me and a great means of support. From there I studied at UCLA and AFI, did coverage and analysis for several production companies for a while, continued to write, act and produce plays and scripts. I then went out on my own as a script doctor.

Is recognizing good writing something you think can be taught or learned?

Absolutely – for both. The "craft", to me, comes first. Learning about story, character development and structure–how to turn an idea into 110 pages of course, is the gig here. So in order for me to recognize it, I had to learn it. I had to discover what structure does, why and how–what makes great story points and all of the rest. When you are reading tons of scripts and attending workshops and seminars by a lot of the great teachers like I have, the recognition of good writing becomes second nature because you're also seeing bad writing and discovering why.

Writers who want to grow and become better intuitively know they need some help. My job is to provide that while showing them their promise as well. Their promise is what we develop. Writers who are open to and then apply good notes will see right off how it betters the work—this is "being taught".

What do you consider the components of a good script?

A memorable story, clear and fresh characters and building structure as I mentioned above, but for most of us, that's a given. Good scripts need to be engaging and surprising too.

Stories that emotionally move you as well as make you feel that you are there. The mark of great writing is a piece that has the reader or audience invested and rooting, one way or the other – eliciting an emotional response. Even though readers may not identify with the situation, they will identify with the emotional life of what the character is going through, the actions and the way the characters behave, and this is because of the human experience.

What I consider the most important component of all of this is that the writer tell the story in a fashion that only her or she could — their own unique voice. This is who they are and how they see the world that nobody else does. The first thing I look at when reviewing a script is the description and I ask myself, "is this textbook or is this from a perspective that I've never seen before?" A script that has a unique and personal voice to it is already leagues ahead as the writer understands not just story, but "their" story and how to get that across.

What are some of the most common screenwriting mistakes you see?

Lack of prep and what's worse, thinking that you don't need it. Okay, great ideas make great stories but only if the idea is turned into a script that encompasses the story and structural elements to evolve, build, grow, sustain and resolve in 110 pages.

Another mistake is writing "pot-boilers", that is, trying to copy what is out there without having a believably sustaining basis for the human aspect. Without a strong and personal character take, motivation, true want and need, you're writing purely externals. Externals don't get it for me. I need to know why.

Another mistake is that Act Two putters out and the scenes begin to get episodic and meandering. Biggest one is protagonist trade-offs: The protagonist, because of lack of drive, stakes, want and need is passive so the action is progressed by secondary characters thus confusing the lines and creating tangential sub-plots that do not correspond with the concept or original goal of the protagonist. I am a big proponent of using an outline. Sure, you could waver from it, but do so in the context of the story that you are now familiar with—this is true and correct inspiration. Write an outline or treatment and get notes on that first. You'll save yourself not only time but ego deflation and bouts of self-doubt. All comes down to execution on the page.

What story tropes are you just tired of seeing?

I'd have to say voice-over as it's so overused. If you're going to use a narrator, and this goes for all devices and conventions, ask how is this still serving the story yet different, adding, and, could it only come from me? Is the narrator a character? Do they know the ending? Are they commenting in a way that goes against the cliché? Are they oblivious, dumb, judgmental? Are they an active character? Also, mentors who are older and have it somewhat together.

Photos on the wall or mantle showing who the characters were and what they did before we see them. I feel that exposition should be meted out when essential and in story forwarding form in crucial times and scene beats.

Lastly, villains that are too dark and mean. My take is that antagonists and villains are the protagonist in their own story; they're just at cross-purposes with the hero. If you can show why antagonists do what they do and their reasoning, it'll be more interesting. Watch the original FRANKENSTEIN bopping and stumbling all over the place, and tell me you don't feel for him.

What are some key rules/guidelines every writer should know?

Write dialogue that differentiates the character as per who they are, their world, POV and experiences. Dialogue that only they could say.

Make sure it's your world; your voice; your take—only you could have written this. The hook, the take, the scenario and the point of view could have only come from you. Not just overall conflict but inner scene conflict between the characters needs to be present evolving and resolved in some fashion, especially if they're on the same side. Individual stakes and progressive character function is vital.

Do not have a character if he or she does not only have a role but also a function. How are they influencing the story and the hero? What happens to turn the story because of them?

Keep us guessing. Great scripts set up surprises, twists and reversals that catch readers off-guard yet make sense as per the foreshowing early on. There is no such thing as "out of the blue" (some comedies and farce exempt) even if you think it is. Everything that happens in Act Three is foreshadowed in some way and credible to this story.

Be open to changes; be open to collaboration; be open to notes that are going to improve the vision overall. Screenwriters are subjective and we need another pair of eyes that are not our own. We need to understand that getting sold, published and produced demands active collaboration. Get notes, shut up or drive a bus. Keep writing. This is a process and you learn as you go. Will you get better at it as you go? Probably. Will you evolve as a writer? Absolutely.

Have you ever read a spec script that was an absolute, without-a-doubt "recommend"? If so, what were the reasons why?

Yes. I reviewed a coming of age drama, a TV pilot, that looks at one night in the lives of several late-teen/early 20's pizza delivery-service workers, concurrently and from all of their points of view. So different were the characters yet all dealing with their own private teen angst. Phenomenal use of subtext; great devices and conventions that were imaginative, unseen before yet fell right in line with the voice and concept.

This slice of life story very convincingly depicted the trials of young adults searching for love but settling for sex and left me with the feeling of hope and the promise of their journeys to come. Because this pilot opened up so many possibilities for all four of the leads, I felt it could go for many episodes and progress uniquely as well. Great writing.

How do you feel about screenwriting contests? Worth it or not?

Only if you do well. Screenwriting contests can help leverage a career but again, you need to have a good script that is recognized by the contest. Bigger question is how are you going to get your script out there? Contests are simply one road and not for all of us.

How can people find out more about you and the services you provide?

You can check out my website at www.storybuilderswrite.com. I'm also on Twitter at @Storybuilderz and on LinkedIn at https://www.linkedin.com/in/storybuilders/

I also have a new e-book entitled THAT SOUNDS LIKE ME – IMPLEMENTING YOUR OWN UNIQUE VOICE INTO ACT I OF YOUR SCREENPLAY OR TV SCRIPT. The book takes a comprehensive approach to the usual refrains on getting your life and slant on the page. By delving into how the writer's natural voice need influence all aspects of the process, it demonstrates how story tools such as Opening Image; Character Construction; Backstory and Exposition; Hooks; Allegories, Metaphors and Themes work together, complement each other, are part of the same world and why. Go to my website and sign in and I'll send you the book for free, as a gift to you.

Readers of this blog are more than familiar with my love/appreciation of pie. What's your favorite kind?

Ha! I'm going to bend the genre here and go with New York Cheesecake – graham cracker crust and bottom.

Jim Mercurio/The Craft of Scene Writing

Originally posted: Feb 1 2019

Jim Mercurio is a writer, author, screenwriter, and filmmaker. His book THE CRAFT OF SCENE WRITING is the first-ever screenwriting book that focuses solely on scenes. He has directed and produced five feature films, and helped countless writers as a teacher, story analyst, and script doctor. He directed more than 40 DVDs on screenwriting, including his own 6-disc set, COMPLETE SCREENWRITING. One of the country's top story consultants, Jim works with Oscar-nominated and A-List writers as well as beginners.

Author's note 1 – a Q&A with Jim was featured in a series of interviews with script consultants that ran on this blog between 2014 and 2015 (and can be found in Volume 1 of this book)

Author's note 2 – full disclosure: Jim played the role of adviser/sounding board for the rewrite of my guardian angel comedy spec

What was the inspiration/motivation for this book?

I believe writers must figure out what is special about what they do and focus on it. Find their voice. I feel like it is the same way with me and the book. I wanted to write a book that was special and that could only come from me.

I have always focused on the nitty-gritty of craft. Probably because I worked so hard trying to figure it out for myself as a writer. My experience as a filmmaker has always informed my approach to understanding and teaching screenwriting. I also wanted to write something that hadn't been done before. I'm not sure why it didn't come to me sooner. I had an "A-ha!" or better yet a "Duh!" moment — SCENE WRITING!

There are a lot of screenwriting books out there. What makes this one unique?

The obvious distinction is that it focuses solely on scene writing... the first screenwriting book to do so.

I was fortunate enough to have story gurus Richard Walter and Michael Hauge review the book. Something Michael said really touched me. He said that there were a lot of ideas in the book he hadn't even thought of. I wanted to cover new ideas or at least some seldom taught concepts in a novel way.

Having been in the screenwriting education niche writing for CREATIVE SCREENWRITING, directing, creating 50 hours of educational DVDs and working as a consultant, I know what's out there. I believe this book will carry the torch and be among the next go-to books for future generations of screenwriters entering the field.

As I mentioned, my filmmaking experience and the fact that I am actively writing screenplays and making projects impacts my perspective. I try to be very specific in my examples. For a given topic, I may start with theory, but I always try to end with concrete principles and tools that you can apply to your writing on the spot.

Some books are geared more towards covering the screenwriting basics, while others "go beyond (or way beyond) the basics". Is this a book that both new and experienced writers could use?

I feel very strongly that this book will appeal to writers across a wide spectrum of skill levels. A friend of mine said I teach the last hundred pages of "the screenwriting book" more than I do the first hundred. This shouldn't be the first book a beginner reads, but for everyone else it's a book you will come back to again and again.

The only research I did while writing this book was to watch movies and think about them. Each chapter is like a stand-alone piece on topics such as exposition, concept, theme, and rewriting. I tried to begin with my, at least somewhat, original and basic take on a topic to ease the reader in and to orient them.

A new writer can jump right in. More advanced writers might recognize my approach as somewhat novel. I then try to go as deep as I can with the material, so that even professional writers might benefit. A writer who read the book said that 70-80% of it was stuff he had never heard before. He might be overstating it, but I'm proud that the book feels that way. I wanted to offer new insight into the nitty-gritty challenge of craft.

Even though the book's title is THE CRAFT OF SCENE WRITING, what else does it cover besides writing scenes?

At its essence, scene writing is storytelling and the same principles apply. You are poring over characters, characterization, idiosyncrasies of the world, setups – to create reversals. You've heard of turning points, right? Writers have to turn a story. They also have to learn how to turn a scene. Or a line of dialogue.

However, I wanted this to complement all of the other screenwriting books that cover story structure. I am looking at screenplays at the molecular level. In the final section of the book, I cover rewriting in a parallel way to how I discuss scene structure. And then I explore how to discover and use your personal voice in your screenplays.

One of the phrases you really emphasized during the process with my script was "write to concept." Can you elaborate on what you mean by that?

Whew, no softballs here. Making me earn my pie.

There are 7500 words in my chapter on concept, which have been through the wringer with my 18 copyeditors, so I explain it better there. But I will try.

Like I mentioned, as a writer you should use what's special about yourself and your writing. Writing to concept means that you are using what's special about your story as the main inspiration for its surprises. For fun, consider a 3-D horror movie where an axe flies across the screen left to right. Do you see how on some level that's just wrong? It should be flying *toward* the camera.

Otherwise, it's ignoring the most prominent element of its medium.

Of course, I'm not that rigid, but writers must narrow down the handful of elements that are essential to their concept because not only do their surprises spin out of them, but, for the most part, they spin out only from them. Writing to concept allows you to find a unique way to express what otherwise might be a familiar story beat. Based on their concept, the moments will look very different. In MEMENTO, Natalie hurts Leonard by hiding pencils. In HER, Samantha, an operating system, hurts her lover by telling him she's in love with 641 other people.

Another of your favorite phrases during the writing process was "go deeper." What should that mean to a writer?

It refers to a missed opportunity to get at more emotion with a character or to complicate a relationship, which would hopefully do the same. While we were working on your script, there's a scene I pointed out featuring a moment where you were on the verge of discovering a powerful and transcendent moment, but then it was all over too soon. Sometimes writers hit a beat (in the broader sense), and maybe they are worried about a looming expansive page count or don't appreciate what they have stumbled upon, so they move on too quickly. They might be better off — pick your metaphor — milking or massaging a moment for a bit longer and letting it play out.

Take a look at the long and emotional monologue in *Good Will Hunting* where Will's best friend Chuckie tells him that he should "cash the winning lottery ticket" and get out of town to find a better life. He even tells him that the best part of the day is in the morning when he comes to pick him up, he has a moment of hope that Will has left — without even leaving a note.

Imagine, if we cut that down to a sentence: "I will miss you but you gotta get the hell out of here." We lose Chuckie's voice, the suspense of it, the emotional heft and importance. It goes from a set-piece scene to a bland, merely functional one.

In addition to the book, you also provide a script consulting service. How can people get in touch to find out more?

Easy. Go to my site at www.jamespmercurio.com. I discuss why coaching is my preferred mode of working with writers. You can check out my DVD set and sign up for info on my classes and free talks.

Last time around, you said your favorite kind of pie was the metaphoric "gross points from my last film". Still the same today, or something different?

A pie in the hand is worth two gross points in a bush. So, hand me some Dutch Apple, please.

Ashley Scott Meyers/Selling Your Screenplay

Originally posted: June 24 2016

Ashley Scott Meyers is a screenwriter and blogger/podcaster at SellingYourScreenplay.com. He has optioned and sold dozens of spec feature film screenplays, with many making it into production. All of Meyers' screenwriting success has come through his own marketing efforts which he teaches on his blog and podcast.

What's the last thing you read/watched that you thought was incredibly well-written?

The screenplay for SOURCE CODE is excellent; one of the best scripts I've ever read. I highly recommend it to anyone who is a screenwriter.

I have two young daughters, ages six and three, so I'm watching a lot of children's movies these days. I just watched THE IRON GIANT for the first time, and thought it was very well-written. In fact, I'd call MEGAMIND one of my favorite films. In terms of screenwriting, it's excellent. There are very few films I watch that I think are perfect, but as a screenwriter, I'd consider it one of the few that could be called practically flawless.

My daughters and I recently watched the 80's classic CLOAK & DAGGER, another very well-written movie. It keeps the action going and all comes together at the end. A very smart script. I saw it when I was a kid and didn't think much of it at the time, but seeing it again, it's a pretty solid piece of writing.

Tell us about your writing background, including your "big break".

I'm not sure I've really had a "big break." Every script I sell or option feels like a monumental effort and it hasn't gotten any easier. In fact, I'd say it's gotten harder as the DVD market has shrunk over the last decade or so.

But to answer your question… I really never had a background in writing. I just liked movies, and for some reason writing scripts appealed to me. So I decide to pursue screenwriting. I was a terrible student when it came to English, writing, spelling, and grammar. Pretty much every skill you need to be a writer, except one (maybe two)… persistence and determination. So I've just plugged away and sold a few scripts.

How did the Selling Your Screenplay blog and podcast come to be?

Believe it or not, I once saw Gary Vaynerchuck speak at a conference where he was talking about not putting your personality into your brands. At the time, I was running a whole bunch of websites, but nothing around screenwriting. So I decided then and there that I needed to do something that combined two of my skills and interests: screenwriting and web development. So I did.

As far as the podcast goes, I started to listening to podcasts and thought they were really powerful. So I launched my own.

You've had experience with short films. What do you consider the benefits of working on a short, both as a writer and filmmaker?

The biggest thing is that you get to see your work get completed, which is rare as a screenwriter. But if you write a halfway-decent short, it's fairly easy (nothing is every easy in this business, but it is possible) to find someone who wants to shoot it. You also might get an IMDb credit, win an award at a film festival, and meet other filmmakers. Shorts are a great way to hone your craft. You're not going to make any money doing them, but they can be a great learning experience.

Is recognizing good writing something you think can be taught or learned?

Yes. The more screenplays you read, and the more you write, the more you'll be able to recognize good writing.

One of the things that makes movies so vibrant is the fact that you can watch a movie or read a script and notice different things every time, depending on where you are in your own life and skill level.

But yes, everyone can get better at writing and recognizing good writing.

What are the components of a good script?

That's a pretty broad question. If I had to boil it down, I'd say good writing evokes genuine emotion in the reader or watcher. If someone reads your screenplay, and it evokes emotion in them, you're on the right track. Everything else, like structure, characterization, dialogue, the hook, theme, etc., is really secondary to being able to evoke emotions in people with your words.

What are some of the most common mistakes you see?

The biggest mistake is underestimating the amount of work it takes to be a professional writer. I hear from so many people who've written one script, entered it into a handful of contests, and then wonder why they haven't made it as a professional writer. Nobody gets to pitch for the Yankees after spending one summer practicing. Being a professional screenwriter is probably as hard as, or at least harder than, being a professional athlete. It takes an enormous amount of luck, talent, and lots and lots and lots of hard work.

What story tropes are you just tired of seeing?

It's often inevitable that you'll write scenes that feel familiar. I often find myself doing it, so I step back and just mix things up a bit. Try anything that'll give the tired tropes a new interesting spin, which often boils down to adding a quirky or interesting character to the scene who can mix things up.

I recently watched a short film where a little girl dropped an ice cream cone that fell to the ground in slow motion. It was so clichéd that I really wondered why the filmmaker didn't try to do something more original.

What are the 3 most important rules every writer should know?

There are really only two mandatory things to do to be a successful screenwriter: write a lot, and read a lot of screenplays. That's it. If you do those two things and really spend time analyzing your writing and the writing of others, you'll get better and maximize whatever talent you have.

How do you feel about screenwriting contests? Worth it or not?

Contests are great. Screenwriters should be doing everything within their power to get their work out into the world, and contests can be a part of that plan. But understand that even winning the best contest still means you're quite a ways away from being a professional screenwriter. And I certainly wouldn't use contests as my only way to market my material.

How can people find out more about you and Selling Your Screenplay?

I blog and podcast over at SellingYourScreenplay.com. I release a new screenwriting podcast episode every week. In nearly every episode, I interview an experienced screenwriter. I also run a script consulting service.

Readers of this blog are more than familiar with my love/appreciation of pie. What's your favorite kind?

Apple. Not very original, I know. But every once in a while someone will bring an apple pie to Thanksgiving dinner, and as I eat it I think, "Damn, that's good pie."

Ellexia Nguyen/The Script Joint

Originally posted: Feb 21 2020

Ellexia Nguyen is the founder of The Script Joint, an award-wining script coverage and editing company. Industry-wise, she started out as an apprentice film editor for producer Roger Corman's company, Concord-New Horizons, and later as an assistant for Paramount Pictures' Worldwide Feature Film Publicity.

After completing UCLA's Professional Screenwriting Program for graduates, she launched her own business. Her company later won the 2016 award for "Script Consultants of the Year" and "Best Screenplay Editing Services"— which is showcased on the U.S. Business News website.

Ellexia works mainly as a script doctor/ghostwriter/story consultant on feature film scripts, TV pilots, TV series bibles, and novels. Some of her clients include directors, attorneys, CEOs of multimedia companies, indie producers, A-list producers, repped writers and some of Amazon's best-selling authors.

Through her story consulting, editing and rewriting services, a handful of her clients, even new writers, successfully reached their goals by leaps and bounds, landing book deals, development deals, and multi-picture deals—some with major studios and streaming companies such as Netflix. Most notably, one of the feature film scripts that she script doctored for a client got picked up by Creative Artists Agency.

What's the last thing you read or watched that you thought was incredibly well-written?

THE ACT, a gripping crime drama series on HULU. I was pulled into the story within minutes of watching the first episode at one of the TV Academy screenings. It's an eerie dramatization of the true story about the murder of Dee Dee Blanchard, a single mom who suffered from MSP (Munchausen Syndrome by Proxy). For those unfamiliar with MSP, it's a psychological disorder where the caretaker, usually the mom, makes up illnesses or does things to induce illnesses in the child under her care. It was a well-told story, and beautifully shot in a way to allow the audience to see and feel what the lead characters were going through.

How'd you get your start in the industry?

Some years ago, I was reading an article in a magazine about director Martin Scorsese and it talked briefly about how he had worked with producer Roger Corman.

After doing some research, I learned that Roger Corman's company, Concorde-New
Horizons, was known for being an informal hands-on film school. After college, I reached out to the company and got an apprentice film editor position. That's where I first came into contact with industry scripts and dailies. Over time, I became more interested in screenwriting.

Is recognizing good writing something you think can be taught or learned?

Yes, if you have a patient script consultant or mentor who is willing to point out to you what makes good writing or not. To recognize good writing, you also have to know how to recognize not-so-good writing. As a script doctor/consultant, I've worked with clients who had little screenwriting and novel book writing background. But over a few months, after giving them proper guidance and extensive story feedback, they were able to dramatically improve their writing and storytelling skills.

As a result, even some new screenwriters and novelists were able to get book and development deals from the drafts we worked on. So, yes, it can be taught – if the person you're teaching has the desire, drive and determination to learn.

What do you consider the components of a good script?

A well-constructed story. Everything has to work together seamlessly such as the cast of characters, dialogue, and the story stakes. For example, a car can have the best engine, but it's not going to take you where you want to be if you have flat tires. In screenwriting terms, that would be like having a good story premise, but characters that can't drive the story forward due to poor dialogue.

Everything counts in a script.

It must have good dialogue because dialogue creates plot. The scenes must be succinctly narrated, moving your story along in a meaningful and visually engaging manner. You want the reader to be able to easily follow and understand your characters and their struggles. Also, the script should be well-paced and filled with a good amount of conflict and story stakes.

Secondary characters should also interact with the main characters without appearing contrived. Lastly, the script should have entertainment value.

What are some of the most common screenwriting mistakes you see?

Having too many secondary characters in the story that end up robbing screen time from the protagonist and antagonist. They're usually secondary characters that interrupt the story and do random things to each other. This often happens in underdeveloped comedies.

In a time-travel story premise, a common mistake is flooding the script with countless arbitrary "time jump" scenes—chaotically jetting back and forth between the past and present. This makes it impossible for the reader to become emotionally invested in any of the characters or their journey.

In sci-fi, it's not sticking to the rules of the writer's own created reality and letting characters do things that contradict the rules of the writer's created reality.

In action, thrillers, and horrors, a common mistake is having an anti-climactic showdown between the hero and the villain. For example, the hero effortlessly defeats the villain, which takes the thrill and momentum out of the fight.

What story tropes are you just tired of seeing?

Like I mentioned earlier, sci-fi stories where the characters have to travel back in time to face something or do something to correct the past in order to save the future. Often times, there are so many time jump scenes such that they interrupt the narrative drive of the story.

What are some key rules/guidelines every writer should know?

Write visually engaging scene descriptions, but don't over- or under-describe.

Give the protagonist clear goals and something to fear. What do they need to overcome to achieve those goals?

Make sure there's a good amount of tension and conflict in the story.

Reward the audience for following your story by making the ending satisfying.

Let your characters speak in subtexts, but try not to be too vague or ambiguous. Script readers aren't mind readers.

Have realistic expectations. Don't expect film investors to shell out millions of dollars to turn your script into a movie if you're unwilling to invest the time and effort to get your script polished. Show them why your script – and not your competitor's – is seriously worth the investment.

Have you ever read a spec script that was an absolute, without-a-doubt "recommend"? If so, what were the reasons why?

Yes, the story unfolded like a movie within minutes. Strong presentation of theme. I was easily able to picture the characters, who seamlessly worked together to serve the plot. Scenes were written in a way to allow me to really see and feel what each of the characters was going through.

How do you feel about screenwriting contests? Worth it or not?

It's one of the ways to test out your script before pitching it to producers. It's also a way to get discovered by literary managers looking for fresh talent. But be selective and don't blindly submit to countless contests. Not all of them offer you the same exposure or "prizes" if you win.

How can people find out more about you and the services you provide?

They can visit www.TheScriptJoint.com, follow us on Twitter at @The ScriptJoint, or connect with me on Facebook – https://www.facebook.com/thescriptjoint

Readers of this blog are more than familiar with my love/appreciation of pie. What's your favorite kind?

Old-fashioned apple.

Rick Ramage/The Screenplay Show

Originally posted: June 17 2016

Rick Ramage is a writer, director and producer with numerous credits on major motion pictures and television shows. During his 25-year career as a screenwriter, he has set up or sold over 40 scripts in Hollywood.

Rick's latest project is The Screenplay Show, a 10-part online series to educate about the art, craft and business of screenwriting and storytelling.

What is The Screenplay Show, and what inspired you to do it?

The Screenplay Show is an actual show about writing, presented in a fun, narrative style. It's a ten-part web series that will focus on the trade secrets I've developed (and learned) from Hollywood's most talented writers, directors and producers during my 25-year career.

As to what inspired it, a few years ago, a buddy of mine started a writer/actor group called, "Write to Act" and he asked me to put on a seminar for his people in Denver. I was reluctant to say the least. For the last 25 years, my only job has been writing and producing film and television. Speaking in public? Not so much.

He kept twisting my arm and after about a year of hounding me, I finally gave in and promised him I would do a one-day seminar. Then reality hit me: What could I possibly say for six hours that would interest other writers and actors? In an effort to alleviate the poor souls who would be stuck looking at my ugly mug all day, I pulled in my editor and we put together a long list of writing samples and clips covering every element of screenwriting so they could actually SEE what I was talking about – instead of listening to me pontificate as I clumsily tried to explain it.

For instance, using stills from THE SHINING, I put every moment of Jack's character arc into a still photo sequence. You can actually visually track his descent into madness. I then put the page number from the script beside each expression. The audience literally gasped, because it was the first time they had actually seen a character arc moment by moment. I did the same thing for all the other elements of storytelling.

As screenwriters, we have to write visually – so I figured it would work for seminars, too. But one thing really surprised me: the audience had as many questions about the writing experience as they did about the nuts and bolts. Personally, I've always been fascinated by the methods of actors, athletes, and other writers, so I guess it's fair that they wanted to know about my method – and how a life and career in the film business actually works.

What sets The Screenplay Show apart from other online seminars?

One look at the teasers we're putting out there will let people know this isn't your father's seminar. I can't honestly say I had an epiphany and The Screenplay Show was suddenly born. But doing the seminars over the next year or two, it definitely evolved into a rolling narrative; my personal Hollywood experience merged into describing actual methods that have worked for me and many of my colleagues. So far, I've set up or sold over 40 scripts.

But I have to give credit where credit is due: I didn't learn how to survive the biz, or sell scripts from books. I learned from working closely with tremendously gracious agents, managers, producers, directors, executives and actors who were generous enough to share their knowledge with me for one purpose – to get the story right.

My goal with The Screenplay Show is to share what they've taught me with other writers and storytellers. And when I say storytellers, I mean anybody involved in the film and television business. Directors, actors, producers, cinematographers, and even executives. They are storytellers because they impact the script and help bring it to life.

Tell us a little about your writing background. How did you get started?

I didn't finish my degree. Instead I went into business with my dad, selling tractors. But I wanted to be well-read and well-spoken, so I sat down with 100 of the great novels and voraciously read them back-to-back. In the process, I began to see how the authors worked the elements. The storytelling process fascinated me. So when I was out covering my sales territory, I began to daydream about becoming a writer.

Eventually, I tried to write a novel. Long story short – it sucked. But the person who told me it wasn't very good also told me I was a good writer. That seemed like a contradiction, but it wasn't. He told me I had a very visual style, and suggested I write a screenplay. So I turned my bad novel into a bad screenplay! (But that process lit a fuse in me, and I've never looked back.)

What have you recently read or watched that you thought was incredibly well-written?

When I'm deep into writing one of my own scripts, I don't usually watch or read much. By the end of the day, more words and plot lines are the last thing I need to relax. But two shows I try not to miss are GAME OF THRONES and HOUSE OF CARDS. From their production values, to the great characters, to the tight, well-structured scripts, I admire them both a great deal. In fact that's how I can tell when I'm in the hands of great storytellers – they make me forget I'm a writer. I become a fan.

Is recognizing good writing something you think can be taught or learned?

Definitely. Recognizing good writing can and certainly should be taught and learned. I've known some executives who were by no means writers, yet they learned to identify good writing and write smart notes. Their jobs depend on it. I've learned to recognize good writing by the way it makes me disappear into it.

What do you consider the components of a good script?

For me, the single most important component of a good script is simply this: It must have soul. I need to feel what the writer is trying to say through his or her characters. If that happens, I know the other elements are working.

What are the three most important rules a writer should know?

<u>Dialogue:</u> When to shut up and let the subtext play.

<u>Action:</u> When not to overwrite. (more often than not, you'll lose your reader.)

<u>Characters:</u> We write in search of ourselves. (makes them real.)

How can people find out more about The Screenplay Show?

We're really encouraging people to go to their most comfortable social media site and follow us.

Also, we're really hoping they go to www.thescreenplayshow.com and sign our landing page. We won't bombard you with trivial junk, but we do want to build a steady audience so we can let people know about events and new material.

Readers of this blog are more than familiar with my love/appreciation of pie. What's your favorite kind?

My grandmother made the best pie I've ever had. Golden, flaky crust made from scratch, crisp green apples sliced thin, and lots of cinnamon! I do miss that woman.

Bob Saenz/That's Not The Way It Works

Originally posted: Jan 10 2020

Bob Saenz is a screenwriter, actor and author. His produced works include Hallmark's HELP FOR THE HOLIDAYS, RESCUING MADISON, SWEET SURRENDER, ON THE TWELFTH DAY OF CHRISTMAS, SOUND OF CHRISTMAS, THE RIGHT GIRL, CHRISTMAS IN LOVE, the theatrical CHURCH PEOPLE, and the black comedy thriller EXTRACURRICULAR ACTIVITIES. He does rewrites and polishes on film and TV projects for producers and production companies. His screenwriting book THAT'S NOT THE WAY IT WORKS was released in 2019.

His acting roles include a 6-year run recurring character run on the TV show NASH BRIDGES, Hallmark's VALLEY OF LIGHT, Francis Ford Coppola's JACK, David Fincher's ZODIAC, Finn Taylor's UNLEASHED, CHURCH PEOPLE, and THE VILLAGE BARBERSHOP, among dozens of others. He was a radio DJ on KYCY-FM in San Francisco, played the last 10 years in the 60's rock band The BSides, and has done voice work on video games, documentaries, and commercials.

Author's Note – I've had the pleasure of knowing Bob personally. His insight and advice has proven invaluable to helping me become a better writer, both in terms of craft and career.

What's the last thing you read or watched that you thought was incredibly well-written?

A spec script by a writer named Rene Gutteridge called WHERE THE WIND COMES. Maybe the best spec I've ever read. Just spectacular. Was emotionally affected by it. Stunning.

What was the inspiration/motivation for your book THAT'S NOT THE WAY IT WORKS?

Two things. One, I've been teaching and speaking at writers' conferences all over the country the last few years and everyone who was there speaking had a book, except me. I complained to my wife about it and she said, "What's stopping you from writing one?" So I did.

Two, there's not a single one I could find out there that spoke plainly about the business of being a screenwriter.

With so many screenwriting books out there, what is it about this one that makes it unique?

The tone. It's conversational. My experience. It's filled with what I have learned actually succeeding at it. With more than a dozen films produced, I used all that experience to write about what I know. And, I talk firsthand about the business of screenwriting. What the writer needs to know about that part of it, which is just as important as writing a script, and how to approach that.

While the first half of the book is about the actual writing of a script, the second half covers the not-as-discussed "what happens AFTER the script is written (i.e. the business aspects)". What advice would you give to writers who want to learn more about this?

As I say in the book – find out that it's not easy, it's not instant gratification, and you have to work at it. Hard. You can succeed; it just takes time and a business plan. I think the book helps with that. Realizing that writing a script is only the beginning of your journey is a BIG eye-opener for most writers who dream of doing this.

Yes, the script needs to be something people would want to choose to see and has to be good, but that's not the end of it.

The book has a great chapter about dealing with rejection. What are some key takeaways and advice you'd offer to writers?

The main takeaway is that rejection isn't personal. Producers and reps don't care enough about you to make it personal. It's ALL about the content. Whether they love your script and not or can use it at that time or not. There are hundreds of reasons to reject a script… you have zero control and it's not personal. Even the most famous screenwriters get rejected on a regular basis. It's an everyday occurrence. You have to learn to live with it or it'll destroy you.

Another important issue writers tend to overlook is the need to effectively market themselves in addition to their script. While the chapter about what NOT to do is entertaining (and a bit eye-opening), what are your suggestions about what writers SHOULD DO?

Use the avenues that producers and reps have opened to the writer. Querying. Something that is an art unto itself and something I delve into pretty deeply in the book with a whole section on query letters.

Networking. There's a huge section in the book about this. The dos and don'ts. One thing to always remember about networking: It's about building relationships, not using people. People who can help you absolutely know the difference and will run away from you if you try and use them.

Contests. The Nicholl and Austin are the ones who will pretty much always get you reads in LA if you final or win them. I've had friends get their films made doing well in both of these. Neither are easy to do well in because of the sheer number of entries, but they can pay off.

The last way is through referrals, especially to get a rep. If you know a producer or director or star who will refer you... but again, this goes back to networking and having the great scripts to back it up.

What do you consider the components of a good script?

The most important thing is a great story. It also has to be lean and mean. Brevity and white space are your friend. You aren't writing a novel. You want just enough in there to have the reader see the film in their head and to be able to fill in what they want to as they read, engaging them in the story that way. Again, a big section in the book about this.

I will say this: Producers are ONLY looking for STORY. Screenwriters can never forget this. Don't over-complicate the read. You can write a complex story without making it hard to read.

Oh... spelling and grammar are important, too.

What are some of the most common screenwriting mistakes you see?

The main one? Choosing the wrong story to tell. Telling a story no one wants to see. Whether it's not sustainable, not interesting, ridiculous, something that's been done a thousand times before, something you can see every day in TV reruns... there are a million reasons NOT to write this kind of story. You need to go through a pretty thorough checklist (in the book) and make sure it's a viable story before you do the time consuming hard work it takes to write a good script. Why do all that hard work on a story that'll be Dead On Arrival?

Another big mistake I see all the time is writers not doing their research about the topics they choose to write about. Writing things that would never ever happen. You have to ground your script in the reality of the subject matter before you take liberties with it.

What are some key writing guidelines every writer should know?

AIS – Putting your Ass In the Seat. You have to be disciplined. Producers expect you to be disciplined. Good to start doing that at the beginning.

Never give up. This is so hard to do, you'll get discouraged on a regular basis. It's a lot easier to give up than to stick with it because it takes years to succeed. Notice I didn't say it CAN take years; I said it TAKES YEARS, because in every case, it does. You aren't going to be the exception.

Don't cheat on research. Take the time to actually learn about the things you're writing about.
Go out and learn them. A big section in the book about this.

Again.... for emphasis.... choose a story that is viable for producers and audiences. Don't just pull something out of the air and write it.

You're not writing a novel. Leave everything that isn't directly hooked to your story or plot points out of your script. One rule of thumb? You know all those people listed in the credits of a film? It's your job to do everything they don't. You aren't a costume designer or a casting agent or set designer.... or... any of them. They don't ask to write the story, you don't try and do their job.

You've managed to establish and maintain a writing career while living outside of Los Angeles. What are some of the pros and cons about it you've experienced?

Pros: I don't live all that far away (400 miles) and can be at any meeting on a day's notice, so it's been fine for me. I am in LA multiple times a year, sometimes for more than a week at a time. It's expensive... but also my choice. There's a section in the book about moving to LA and when to pull the trigger and do it if you need to.

Con: I'm not in LA networking all the time. Out of sight, out of mind is a real thing. Not worth moving there for me, though.

Readers of this blog are more than familiar with my love/appreciation of pie. What's your favorite kind?

Peach. Nothing else comes close.

Tim Schildberger/Write LA

Originally posted: July 9 2021

Tim Schildberger is an experienced writer, script coach, and co-founder/Head Judge of Write LA (http://write-la.com) – an annual screenwriting competition that gives writers a chance to get read by managers, and hear their winning script read by professional actors in LA (and posted on YouTube). He cares far too much about helping writers improve their craft and get access to the industry. Tim is an expat Australian, a former TV journalist, writer on the globally popular soap opera NEIGHBOURS, newspaper columnist, creator of a comedy/reality series for the Travel Channel called LAWRENCE OF AMERICA, and one of the key members of the original BORAT team. He has stories.

In his spare time, Tim is a husband, parent, tennis player, road tripper, and he and his family foster kittens. Seriously. Twitter: @write_la Instagram: @writela

What was the last thing you read or watched you considered exceptionally well-written?

I hate to be a cliché, but THE CROWN – sets the bar very high. Peter Morgan is a genius. His ability to tell a story with and without words, and build tension in scenes that on the page might appear boring, is remarkable. THE QUEEN'S GAMBIT had similar skill, attaching us to an unconventional character quickly and effectively. Feature films – I loved PALM SPRINGS – structurally, and characters/dialogue, and who doesn't love a woman solving the problems using education and intellect!

How'd you get your start in the industry?

I was 22, living in Australia (where I'm from), working as a trainee TV News Producer. I had applied to newsrooms, and I'd called up various TV series, asking if they needed a writer. It was a simpler time. A nightly soap opera, NEIGHBOURS, let me do a writing submission, which they liked – and said they'd get back to me. In the meantime I got the job in TV news.

One day, six months later, I got a call in the newsroom, it was NEIGHBOURS, asking if I'd like to write an episode. I said yes, obviously. They mailed me the scene breakdowns, I typed my script on a typewriter, and ten days later mailed it back. All after working a full day in the newsroom. I did that 5 more times before it all got far too overwhelming. I was the youngest writer they'd ever had, and that experience made it clear to me that writing, in all its forms, was my future.

What was the inspiration for creating the Write LA competition?

We wanted to create a competition we'd want to enter. I've been writing for a long time – and I've entered competitions large and small. I've won a few, placed in a bunch, and it became clear that many of the writing comps out there don't really do much when it comes to attracting attention, gaining industry access, or launching careers. And pretty much none put any kind of focus on helping writers improve their command of craft. So our goal was to build a competition that somehow combined both goals – to help with the craft, and to help with the access.

What makes Write LA unique compared to other screenwriting competitions?

Two things I think separate us. First, we are a competition run by actual writers. So we are able to deliver a certain degree of respect and admiration for the act of actually finishing a script and entering it – that many competitions lack. We know how it all feels.

Second, we stand proudly in front of the competition. Everyone knows I'm the co-founder and Head Judge. When you email a question, it comes to me. I do an enormous amount of reading, and I'm supervising every aspect of the competition. We try hard not to be a faceless comp where sometimes it can feel like you're sending your script into a void, and then hoping something emerges. It matters to us that the entrants feel 'seen'.

A big concern for writers entering a screenwriting competition is the quality/experience level of its readers. How does Write LA address that?

I hear that. And I've experienced it firsthand. A script will make the Nicholl semifinals, and won't make it out of the first round somewhere else. And then you get 'feedback' that feels like it was written by someone who never actually read the script, they just strung a few buzzwords together.

So to address that – I'm heavily involved in the reading process. I've handpicked our small team, I do a ton of reading personally, and I set pretty clear parameters when it comes to what I'm looking for when it comes to command of craft. Every script that makes it into our top 15 semi-finalists will have been read by at least three different people, including me.

We give every script, whatever the genre, or whether it's a TV pilot or feature, full respect and attention. And all the additional feedback (offered at an extra fee), is done by me personally. So there is a consistency of the feedback, and a name attached to it (mine). I'm not interested in telling anyone what I would do, I'm focused entirely on maximizing the opportunities presented by the writer and doing my best to empower them to bring the most out of their idea, and their skills.

What do you consider the components of a good script?

Gosh – this isn't easy to answer quickly, but I'll try. For me, a good script needs fleshed out characters, who face clear challenges – no matter how big or small. Because no matter how detailed the world, or 'big' the story, if we don't care about the characters, it's all a waste of time.

Also, an understanding of the audience experience is awesome. A writer who is aware of audience expectations, and is able to manipulate those expectations is exciting. And finally, a clear sense of where the story is heading. Not a lot of extra clutter. Just a solid story, competently and confidently told.

What are some of the most common screenwriting mistakes you see?

Misuse of Scene Description is HUGE. Using it to reveal character details an audience couldn't possibly know. Using it to show off a writer's literary command – with all sorts of flowery descriptions that waste time, rather than establish 'mood'.

Not writing an outline. I'm confident I can pick within 5 pages if a writer has an outline, and a firm idea of who this story is about, and where it is going. And taking too long to dive into story. Spending page after page building a complicated world, and then finally starting some sort of story – is a big mistake. Even STAR WARS had a brief title explanation, and then we were into Darth Vader storming Leia's ship. The rest we figure out as we go.

Lastly, I have to add too many spelling errors. A sloppy script does not inspire confidence.

What story tropes are you just tired of seeing?

A character waking up, turning off their alarm, and getting into the shower as the first thing we see. Happens WAY more often than you would expect, and is not only dull, but unwise. What viewer who sits in a darkened movie theatre wants to see a feature film start that way?

I'm also not a fan of drawn out action sequences. It's great that you see the car chase in your head, but all a reader cares about is 'does someone important die?'

Oh, and a shot of 'overdue bills' on the kitchen table. Anything but that please. I see a lot of stereotypes with the characters too – which usually tells me a writer is basing a character on another character they've seen in a movie or on TV – rather than an actual, flawed, complex human being.

What are some key rules/guidelines every writer should know?

What you are doing is more about hard work than flashes of inspiration. It's less about talent than it is about grind.

Accept that re-writing is inevitable. Your first draft will not be a work of art. It's a starting point.

Learn to receive notes as comments on the words on a page, not a personal attack, or a statement on your writing ability.

Characters are more important than story nowadays. Put the extra effort into figuring out who they are, and their emotional journey through your story.

What you are doing is brave, and awesome, and you should feel very proud of yourself every time you finish anything. Every time. Plenty of people talk about writing something. You went and did it. That's huge and should never be ignored.

There is no work of art in the history of human beings that has ever been loved by 100% of the people. Accept that your work will not be universally loved – because humans are humans.

Details matter. Every scene matters. Every line of dialogue matters. Everything you do is conveying a message to an audience. Understand and embrace that.

Have you ever read a script where you thought "This writer really gets it"? If so, what were the reasons why?

I read many scripts like that! I read hundreds of scripts a year, so I regularly find writers who are very skilled. As for reasons, I would say the absolute, clear number one is making me feel something. I'm not alone in this. I tell anyone who'll listen if you can make a reader feel a genuine human emotion, that is FAR more important and impactful than any set piece, world, intricate story or cute scene description. It isn't even close.

Also, it's fun to read scripts by writers who think about the audience, and work hard to provide us with a rich, enjoyable experience. I know the expression "write what you know" is popular. My version is "write what you know, but make it accessible to strangers."

And while I'm here, let me add that writing what you know really refers to your emotional experience and authenticity. Not your time in middle school. If you can dig into your emotional space, which is uniquely yours, and share that on the page – that authenticity connects you with a reader/audience, and goes a long way to establishing what the industry likes to call your "voice". I'd like to say it was easy to do. It's not. But it's important.

Readers of this blog are more than familiar with my love/appreciation of pie. What's your favorite kind?

I have to say I'm a big fan of custard. There's a custard tart in my homeland Australia – a mini pie – which is very much my favorite. But as that doesn't really exist here – I'm going to say I like banana cream, apple, peach, and I'm a big fan of all the cobblers and crumbles too. I don't think I'd refuse any pie that came my way.

Travis Seppala/365: A Year Of Screenwriting Tips

Originally posted: Aug 2 2019

Travis Seppala is a Los Angeles-based screenwriter. In addition to selling shorts, optioning features, being hired to write dozens of feature films and episodes of television, he's also published the book 365: A YEAR OF SCREENWRITING TIPS.

What was the thing you read or watched you considered incredibly well-written?

My favorite script of all time was A KILLING ON CARNIVAL ROW. I'm thrilled to see it's being turned into a series on Amazon, and will be very interested to see how the format changing from feature to TV affects the amazing story.

I think the perfect movie is IT HAPPENED ONE NIGHT. It might be a little corny by today's standards, but a lot of it (both story and dialogue) still holds up today.

And for TV, we're in the new golden age where almost everything is super well-written! One of my current favorites is DOOM PATROL. It's about a superhero team, but it's also a deeply emotional drama. It just happens to be about misfits with powers (and problems).

What do you consider the components of a good script?

Compelling (i.e. interesting and fun) story.

3-dimensional characters who are the right people to partake in the compelling story.

Terse, snappy descriptions.

Lots of white space.

Connectivity (i.e. everything makes sense and flows smoothly).

What was the inspiration/motivation for your book 365: A YEAR OF SCREENWRITING TIPS?

Facebook! I'm in a bunch of screenwriting forums on Facebook. There are both experienced writers and total newbies on there. A lot of the newbies, though, seem to keep asking the same questions over and over and over and over and over and over and... you get the point. Many of their questions make it seem like they forget Google is even a thing.

After a while, seeing repeated questions and questions that can be answered with about five seconds of research on Google, I thought "What if all these answers were in one place, by category?"

I figured I could put it all together, plus answer a bunch of questions that aren't being asked. And so the book was born.

There are a lot of screenwriting books out there. What about this one makes it unique?

Many of those other books are about a specific aspect of screenwriting. Story. Character development. Rewrites. Business.

365: A YEAR OF SCREENWRITING TIPS runs the gamut of covering ALL aspects of screenwriting, from before you have an idea to after you sell a script and everything in between…. all in bite-size tips!

Its purpose isn't to try and make you "better" in any specific thing. And I don't claim to be a guru or expert; I'm just relaying info I've learned either through a ton of book reading or personal experience. The book is just meant to help show you the ropes, and makes suggestions on different ways to look at things. Try a bunch of stuff and see what works for you!

Plus, there's a bunch of coupons for discounts and freebies on a lot of helpful products and services!

Some screenwriting books are geared more towards covering the basics, while others "go beyond (or way beyond) the basics". Is this a book that both new and experienced writers could use?

The book is geared more toward beginning writers, but my hope is that experienced writers will find some new concepts and suggestions useful as well. Even experienced writers should always be learning.

With 365 tips to choose from, are there any that really seem to resonate with readers? Or any that always instigate an argument?

A couple that have gone over well with people are my tips on creating a positivity calendar (because it's far too easy to get wrapped up in all the negative aspects of this life) and playing The Comp Game (a great way to produce new stories that are "similar but different").

The big one that's gotten people upset is Tip #1: Experts Are Liars!

There's one section in the book called "Before You Start", and one called "Prep Work". What do you consider the difference between the two?

The "Before You Start" section is about things to know before even trying to come up with the idea for a script. It talks about the odds of making it, the fact that there's a lot of conflicting information out there (and even in this book), and things to consider before you ever start on this journey.

"Prep Work" is about... well... prep work! Ideas. Brainstorming. Outlining. Figuring out what to write a script about.

Before You Start = knowing what you're getting into.

Prep Work = getting started.

Part of your own backstory involves your relocating to Los Angeles. Where do you fall in the "You have to live in LA to make it" discussion?

Whether or not you HAVE to be in Los Angeles sort of depends on what you're trying to accomplish in the industry.

If you want to be a television writer, then yes, you absolutely MUST move to LaLa Land! Shows shoot all over the country (and even other countries), but the majority of them have writers rooms in the L.A. Area. How can you expect to get a job if you don't even live where that job is?

Now, if you want to write features? Then you can live anywhere. But expect to make trips to Los Angeles if/when possible. Why? Because you need to take meetings. Meetings with reps, meetings with producers, meeting with studio heads. Sure, it's possible to do phone meetings, and you probably will do a bunch... but nothing beats the in-person impression when selling your work.

As a follow-up to that, how has it been for you and your career since arriving in Los Angeles?

There's been good stuff and bad. Like a lot of transplants, I thought I'd get here and "be discovered" in the first year. That didn't happen. Been here 3 years and still just trying to make it.

I've met LOTS of people, though, and made great connections with other writers, reps, showrunners, producers, crew members, and more! My Rolodex is filled out, and it wouldn't have been if I hadn't come here.

I've also gotten some gigs because I met people at parties out here and hit it off.

The thing to know, though, is that while being here makes it easier to have access to decision makers, it also becomes harder to fit in. You might be the best writer in your small Oklahoma town, but in Los Angeles almost everyone is a damned good writer! It's the "big fish, little pond" situation. The ocean is where it's at, but it's also rougher water.

You offer more than a few tips about networking, especially at social events. How much of an impact has that had for you?

I've gotten jobs from people, made loads of friends, and even met my fiancée (now wife) – all at these kinds of events!

I really enjoyed the final section – "After Your Script Is Done". How much of that is based on your own personal experience?

Much of the book is based on my own experiences in the industry. I don't go into a lot of personal stories or examples of my own material like many screenwriting books do, but my experience is definitely where a lot of my "wisdom" comes from.

However, all the stuff in that section is great advice for any writer. It speaks to Serial Starters, Talented individuals, Procrastinators, Newbies who just make mistakes with what they're writing, Paranoids, Worry-Warts, and Newbies searching for the next steps. There's also some great coupons in that last section, myths busted, and a suggestion for a killer ice cream place!

Apart from writing scripts, you also offer a script consulting service. How can writers get in touch with you to find out more?

email: flannelmann@yahoo.com

Facebook: facebook.com/travisseppala

Twitter: @TravisSeppala

Readers of the blog are more than familiar with my love & appreciation of pie. What's your favorite kind?

My favorite pie has always been Shoofly Pie. It's this super sweet molasses pie that, so far as I can tell, you can only get in Amish country. Sadly, I haven't had it since I was a child. I keep meaning to find a recipe online for it... but... *shrugs* when it comes to pie, I'd rather someone else make it for me.

But for those playing at home, I actually prefer cookies to pie. Sorry.

Marlene Sharp

Originally posted: Dec 13 2019

Marlene Sharp is a creative and business-savvy entertainment multi-hyphenate who originally hails from New Orleans but is now a (San Fernando) Valley girl. Firmly ensconced in LA life, she currently serves as the Head of IP Strategy and Acquisitions for Rainshine Entertainment and its dedicated animation divisions Kinsane (kids and family focus) and Raijin Studios (animation for teens and grown-ups).

Formerly, as Producer, TV Series, at Sega of America, Marlene worked on much more than the Teen Choice Award-nominated Cartoon Network series SONIC BOOM. For example, her Hedgehog duties took her to the heights of nerd-dom as an official San Diego Comic-Con 2017 panelist.

As a freelance journalist, Marlene concentrates on pop culture for buzz-worthy fan destinations, such as DOGTV, ToonBarn.com, Geekified.net, and CultureSonar.com. As a short film auteur, she has snagged recognition at the Kids First! Film Festival, the Canine Film Festival, the San Luis Obispo Film Festival, and many more.

Marlene is the proud winner of 2019 LA Shorts International Film Fest Script Competition (an Oscar and BAFTA-qualifying fest), at which her backdoor sitcom pilot received a staged reading by The Groundlings. And as a human being, she loves dogs. For proof of the aforementioned, please see her website www.pinkpoodleproductions.com.

What's the last thing you read or watched that you thought was incredibly well-written?

I love Shia LaBeouf's screenplay for his autobiographical film HONEY BOY. The storytelling is clever!

Podcasts are a relatively new obsession of mine, and there are a few standout wordsmiths. American Scandal (Lindsay Graham); Broken: Jeffrey Epstein (Adam Davidson, Julie K. Brown); Gangster Capitalism (Andrew Jenks); and Hitman (Jasmyn Morris) immediately come to mind.

How'd you get your start in the industry?

My start in the biz was almost my end in the biz. I was bitten during pre-K and subsequently began serious research on kids in show business. SESAME STREET was the inspiration. It seemed like a neat place to be, and I wanted in. During grade school, I devoured library books about stage moms and such, and then told my mother that I needed an acting agent. She said 'no' and encouraged me to play with my Barbies instead, which I did in earnest. She continued tough love at every turn and for many years. When I declared a Drama/Communications major in college, though, it was time for the Sharp family to face the music . . . and drama!

Is recognizing good writing something you think can be taught or learned?

If one is industrious enough, then one could self-teach. For today's inquisitive, budding writer, there are so many resources (many are free or low cost): books, eBooks, seminars, writers' groups, classes, online classes, podcasts, YouTube videos. Perhaps the best resource, though, is actual content consumption, especially in the genres that one loves best.

What do you consider the components of a good script?

Relatable characters and story, clever dialogue, and an unexpected plot turn or two are elements of my favorite scripts. Good non-sequiturs also tickle me!

What are some of the most common screenwriting mistakes you see?

Spelling and grammar errors abound. They're everywhere!

What story tropes are you just tired of seeing?

I'm really tired of the deus ex machina that recur in garden-variety superhero/fantasy movies, such as the uber hero or uber anti-hero – with his/her signature moves – who appears at the eleventh hour. In my opinion, JOKER is groundbreaking (and therefore entertaining), because it discards the usual clichés.

What are some key rules/guidelines every writer should know?

- Spellcheck.
- Proofread.

- Patience, and lots of it.

Have you ever read a spec script that was an absolute, without-a-doubt "recommend"? If so, what were the reasons why?

Yes! A spec script for THE SIMPSONS by my friend Adam Kosloff. The premise is absurd and hilarious. Adam and his writing partner nail Bart's character; he becomes a grilled cheese celebrity chef. The humor is magical, laugh-out-loud funny. I'll never forget it.

How do you feel about screenwriting contests? Worth it or not?

Definitely worth it! Such cost-effective personal marketing! Highly recommend!

How can people find out more about you and the services you provide?

1) My business website: www.pinkpoodleproductions.com

2) My script and bible doctoring services:
www.wefixyourscript.com

3) My CV: www.linkedin.com/in/marlenesharp

4) A few of my credits: www.imdb.me/marlenesharp

Readers of this blog are more than familiar with my love/appreciation of pie. What's your favorite kind?

A solid tie between pumpkin and chocolate!

Brian Smith/Monument Scripts

Originally posted: May 11 2018

Brian Smith of Monument Scripts grew up on Cape Cod, long a favorite haunt of writers and artists, surrounded by and loving well-told stories. When he left the Cape, it was to study the techniques and principles of good storytelling at the University of Southern California. There he earned an MFA from USC's School of Cinematic Arts.

He began his career in the industry working for Disney, and then Universal, Sony, and DreamWorks Animation, and he has credits on 24 films and television series. Brian's been a professional screenplay reader since 2006, and has written coverage for over 1,000 scripts and books for such companies as Walden Media and Scott Free Films.

Brian currently lives in Los Angeles, with his wife, three daughters and two dogs.

What's the last thing you read/watched that your thought was incredibly well-written?

If we're talking incredibly well-written, I would say the last thing was COCO. Full disclosure here, my background is in animation. I've worked in animation my whole career, but I've been kind of down on Pixar for about the last 10 years or so. I felt like it had been at least that long since they put out a complete film. I thought WALL-E and UP were both half-great films in that the first half of each of them was great, but the other half was mediocre to just bad. Other films that they put out during that stretch, like any of the CARS movies, FINDING NEMO/DORY, or even TOY STORY 3, were really lacking in strong stories. They always had wonderful characters that the audience fell in love with. That allowed for hyper-emotional endings, which was ultimately why those films were so successful.

I thought with COCO, they put everything together in a way that they hadn't since THE INCREDIBLES and RATATOUILLE, and they finally made a complete film. The story was thematically very strong, the stakes were very high, and they gave us a twist at the end I did not see coming. I don't cry during movies, but I had a lump the size of a golf ball in my throat at the end. The quality of the writing in the script had everything to do with that.

How'd you get your start reading scripts?

I fell into it, really. I was working on the CURIOUS GEORGE feature years ago, and we were all about to get laid off as the show was wrapping. One of my co-workers suggested script coverage as a way to make some money while being unemployed, and he put me in contact with a creative executive he knew at Walden Media. I contacted him. He had me do a test, which they liked, and they started sending me work. I fell in love with evaluating stories and writing, and have been doing it ever since.

Is recognizing good writing something you think can be taught or learned?

Absolutely, and it can be both taught and learned. Writing is one of those unique disciplines that's equal parts creativity and technique. You have to use your imagination in order to be a good writer, but you also have to use dramatic structure. Determining the merit or quality of a premise or an idea can be a subjective thing, but evaluating a writer's technique and skill level is absolutely something that can be taught.

What a lot of writers don't understand is that good dramatic structure makes you a better writer. Just as anyone can be taught to implement that structure in their writing, others can be taught to evaluate how successful the writer was in implementing it and how that implementation strengthened or weakened the story.

What are the components of a good script?

A good script is a story well-told; that takes the reader on a journey to a world that the reader can envision and become a part of. In order to do that, a good script needs to have been spawned from a strong premise. A strong premise usually gives way to strong thematic elements, which are also necessary for a good script. A script is almost always better when it has something that it's trying to say.

A strong thematic component is also a way to make us care about the characters, which is probably the most important component. I need to care about the characters and what happens to them. I need to feel some emotional attachment. Without that, you've got nothing.

What are some of the most common mistakes you see?

Not adhering to proper story structure is a big one. The transition from Act II to Act III is one that tends to trip people up the most. Poorly written dialogue is another one. Writing good dialogue is hard, and most writers from whom I get scripts haven't yet mastered the art of subtext, which is crucial to writing good dialogue.

It also seems as though a lot of writers think that big words mean good dialogue, which isn't necessarily the case. Finally, flat characters are a common problem in scripts I get. It's especially problematic and common in protagonists. Many writers are reticent to give their hero a flaw or some other issue that gives him or her depth, and it's so important to do so.

What story tropes are you just tired of seeing?

The post-apocalyptic sci-fi thing. I love science fiction and there have been some great post-apocalyptic stories. There's a reason THE HUNGER GAMES was huge. It was a terrific story with real pathos and drama. Unfortunately, it made way for a lot of other stories that tried to do the same thing, but just didn't do it as well. Even THE HUNGER GAMES went out on a whimper for me as the last movie wasn't nearly as good or as compelling as the first. I had the same opinion of the books as well. But that's a trope I kinda wish would just go away.

What are the 3 most important rules every writer should know?

Story structure, story structure, and story structure.

Have you ever read a script where you could immediately tell "This writer gets it."? What was it about the writing that did that?

Yeah, and it was actually a bit annoying. I was reading for a contest, and got a script written by a woman who was a doctor and a lawyer, and the script was about a woman who was a doctor and a lawyer. I know this is super-petty of me, but I really wanted to hate it because it's really annoying when someone is good and successful at everything they try. But I have to admit it was an exceptional script, with an interesting protagonist, a compelling storyline and meaningful thematic elements, all written in a cinematic style. It was easy to envision this as a courtroom drama worthy of the genre. The writer really understood what it took from a technical standpoint to write a story well, and her personal experiences allowed her to tap into material that was interesting and dramatic.

How do you feel about screenwriting contests? Worth it or not?

I believe it is worth it, especially nowadays. With studios less likely to option or buy spec scripts, doing well in a screenwriting contest might be the best way for some writers to break into the business. And the beautiful thing is, you don't even have to win. You could be just be a finalist, a semi-finalist, or even a quarter-finalist, and there's a good chance someone from a studio is reading your script and could possibly be impressed with your work. Even people who aren't winning these contests are getting meetings that could lead to work.

You might not sell your script this way, but your talent could be recognized by someone who has the power to hire you to write something else, and that could break you into the industry. I personally have a friend that experienced that. She got her script into a couple of contests. She didn't win any of them, but her script caught the eyes of people that could do something with it, and she's been taking meetings and getting offers for representation. So if you have a quality script you can't get past the studios' Threshold Guardians, enter it into a contest, and there's a chance that the studios could be calling you.

How can people get in touch with you to find out more about the services you provide?

People can check out my website: http://monumentscripts.com/ or follow me on Twitter @monumentscripts.

You can also email me directly at briansmi71@gmail.com

Readers of this blog are more than familiar with my love/appreciation of pie. What's your favorite kind?

We must be kindred spirits, because I am definitely a pie guy. I'd rather have pie for my birthday than cake, and will never turn down a slice of pie for anything. That said, I prefer fruit pies to crème pies, and my favorite of all the fruit pies is blueberry. My favorite way to have it is warmed up with vanilla ice cream on top. That is, unless I'm eating it for breakfast. Then it's just plain.

Michael Tabb/Prewriting Your Screenplay

Originally posted: May 18 2018

Michael Tabb is a working screenwriter, decade-long current and active member of the WGA (the Writers Guild of America, West is the Hollywood screenwriters' union), a multiple-award-winning screenwriting educator, and author of a film-festival-winning Best Screenplay.

He's agile enough to write horror for Universal Studios, family for Disney Feature Animation, a period war epic for a production company at Warner Brothers, and has worked with creative icons of all types, from comic-book legend Stan Lee to Academy Award winning actor Dustin Hoffman.

His book, PREWRITING YOUR SCREENPLAY: A STEP-BY-STEP GUIDE TO GENERATING STORIES, explains how he develops great, cohesive script ideas that continue to get him work, released by Focal Press, the entertainment-business division of Routledge, America's #1 textbook publisher.

What's the last thing you read/watched that you thought was incredibly well-written?

I recently watched the Netflix series LOST IN SPACE and felt it did a lot of things right. The characters are really specific and strong, each with really unique qualities that separate them from

GO AHEAD AND ASK - V2

each other. There was constant danger, whether through the hostile environment or the characters that found their way into the family's graces (be they human or robotic). Meanwhile, each episode ends with a new and engaging development that hooks the viewers to binge another episode. Between LOST IN SPACE and STRANGER THINGS, I think Netflix is redefining the kind of television an entire family might gather around the flat screen to watch together.

Were you always a writer, or was it something you eventually discovered you had a knack for?

STAR WARS sparked my imagination, and I was drawing and creating science-fiction stories by the age of six. In middle school, I handwrote ten 20-24-page short-form adventure stories of a starship crew called THE ALLIANCE inspired by STAR TREK. Each chapter was a new mission. I explored superhero and horror spoofs earlier in my high school days until I wrote my first short (44-page) screenplay in a modern, contemporary setting for my final English Lit paper. In short, the more mature I became, the more my stories grew more grounded and closer to reality.

Even though I loved writing, saying I had a knack for it would be far too generous. I was certainly a storyteller, but I was always academically far better at mathematics than English. I did, however, have a knack for drama. I took acting classes at South Coast Repertory and was actively involved in my high school drama program for all four years, participating in every play and musical I could. Acting taught me how important it was to define your character from all the others and to keep the tension at a level high enough to make each scene compelling. Every character had purpose, and it was true no matter what scene or show I was doing. These lessons carry over into writing, but because I wasn't a gifted English student in my formative years, I never would have suspected I could have a career as a writer. I always thought I was going to be a character actor.

It took me many years and tremendous insight from my teachers at USC, NYU, and UCLA to make me a decent writer. They all earned their money. The time I spent analyzing characters and scripts as an actor was very helpful, including studying at the Atlantic Theater Company in NYC, a brainchild of the great American playwright David Mamet. It took a lot of work to understand how to do each aspect of concept creation and execution correctly. The only thing that came naturally is my escapist imagination. The rest was hard-fought, learned, and earned over years of writing and rewriting.

What was the script you'd consider gave you your "big break"?

I want to pause a second to say that I think the cliché of miraculously getting that one big break that changes everything is a terribly unhealthy and damaging fallacy. One opportunity may lead to another, and sometimes it doesn't. Most working writers are constantly "breaking in" over and over again. Anyone who makes a living wage as a creative in this business is fortunate. Just remember, we do this job for our insatiable love of telling great stories. If that's not your goal, it won't be worth the amount of work you have to put into this job. Trust me. People have won Academy Awards and not gotten a job for years afterwards. So, if you get a break, save up so the money lasts the unpredictable draughts and keep writing.

With that said, I'll reply by talking about the script that landed me my first paycheck as a screenwriter.

I was exceptionally lucky that the first screenplay I ever wrote is the one that landed me an agent and my first writing deal. Even so, it didn't happen overnight. It took several years for it to get into the hands of those in Hollywood that could make a difference for me, and I had written around ten scripts between having written my first and setting it up with producers. The option on that screenplay has since expired, and I own that script again. I still wish someone would make it. It's a high-concept swashbuckler in the spirit of SHAKESPEARE IN LOVE, THE THREE MUSKETEERS, and THE PRINCESS BRIDE. It's a fun-spirited, romantic romp set in the south of France full of swords, gallantry, and a sense of humor.

Taking a look at your bio, you've worked in a lot of different genres. Are there any that hold a special appeal to you, and is there a genre you haven't worked in yet, but would really like to try?

I've written in every genre I can think of, most of which were for money, including: rom-com, drama, western, war epic, historical, biopic, science fiction, fantasy, crime, thriller, horror, supernatural, action, and adventure. I love each genre differently and deeply for the gifts each offers us. While I'm very proud of the diversity and breadth of my stories, it has also been my greatest career shortcoming. It would have been a far smoother journey if I picked a lane and stuck with it a bit more, but that's not how I work.

The more you prove yourself a master of one genre in our business, the more people pay you to write it for them. As an example of this in another profession, when an extremely famous comedic actor gets the chance to play a dramatic role, they often take a big hit in the pocketbook. They don't get paid the same as they do in the genre of his or her specialty. Even so, working without constraints and limitations is worth it to me. I have a solid batting average for landing writing jobs on which I get to pitch.

When I decide to write a story about something, I refuse to fit a square peg into a round hole. I'm not going to force my story into a genre because that is my specialty. I would rather pick the genre that I feel will be the best and most poignant reality in which to tell it. The story tells me where it must go. Right now, I'm rewriting two screenplays simultaneously, an ensemble reunion-of-old-friends drama and a supernatural thriller. The project before that, which is still being developed, was a period adventure television show. I love writing period pieces, sci-fi, action, adventure, and anything remotely escapist. I adore them all.

What inspired you to write your book Prewriting Your Screenplay: A Step-by-Step Guide to Generating Stories?

I had kept a long document of all the tricks of the trade that I liked using best. It ran almost three hundred single-spaced pages. I developed my own approach to writing by putting those tricks together in a certain order. Since then, I have never had writer's block.

I work on multiple projects at once, and I've been asked by tons of writers how I do what I do. Though editing takes a while, others have always been blown away by how quickly I can create a strong and cohesive initial draft. They'd take me to lunch and pick my brain. Later, they'd tell me I changed their lives and approach to developing stories.

I adore giving back, helping writers. Helping one person at a time was great, but I felt I could do better. I got more involved at the WGA, putting panels together for the Writers Education Committee, and I co-created the first ever WGA Mentor Program in my spare time. I guest-lectured and spoke when asked in classrooms and served on panels for writer conferences. Finally, I bit the bullet and agreed to teach an actual class online in Full Sail University's online MFA program while still taking writing gigs for companies like Universal Studios. I'm also going to speak at the Central California Writers Conference in late September.

When I was asked to be on a panel for the Screenwriters World Conference in L.A., I told Jeanne Bowerman of Script Magazine about my 284 pages of notes I planned to turn into a book one day when I had the time. She asked me to write some articles I could use as a kind of running start to writing the book about my method. So, I did that to get the ball rolling. As I fleshed those articles into a full-fledged book, Full Sail University liked the published articles I wrote on character creation so much, they asked me to take over the Character Creation and Development portion of their online MFA Creative Writing program. Based on that, I knew I was communicating my method well, and I should finish the book.

I figured the book was the very best way of helping the most writers at once. In short, it all stems from the hope of giving back to my craft. I am only as good as I am because the writers who came before me taught what they had learned. My goal was to take that knowledge another step forward in the hopes that someday my book will not only help others, but it will inspire another great writer to take my ideas a step further as well. In short, human knowledge is all about continuing to construct our Tower of Babel, evolving our art form by working together to save the world.

Yes, I said save the world.

I believe storytelling is how we inspire others to invent amazing technology, see the world from new perspectives, and provide a deeper understanding of humanity. So, teaching others to write better is my way of getting others to create stories that change the way we think. When we change the way people think, we can change the way people will behave and treat one another.

My job as a writer isn't to just tell a cool story and make some money. I wouldn't need to share my tricks if that were my only goal in this trade. Storytelling is an incredibly powerful medium. Think about how it can bring people to euphoric laughter and devastating tears over events that never even happened and characters that don't exist. As Spider-Man has taught us all, with great power comes great responsibility. Writers have the ability to make the world better for having written their stories. If I help other writers be more effective, I could be helping thousands of writers convey their impactful messages, bettering our world through teaching empathy, understanding, and the potential paths forward (or to avoid) in order to achieve a greater tomorrow for us all.

Yes, that makes all of you writers out there potential superheroes.

With so many screenwriting books out there, what is it about yours that makes it especially unique?

I always said if I'm going to write something, it's not going to be something they can find anywhere else done the same way. We can't help but work off of some universally accumulated knowledge, like genre, character types, and three-act structure, but we can strike out on our own by presenting how to assemble them in a new way. The knowledge is all out there, but it's about how you put the pieces together and in what order.

So many screenwriting books call themselves a "step-by-step" guide, but when you try to apply the steps in the order they offer them, it's not a fluid roadmap you can follow to construct a story. It's not really a step-by-step guide. It's a series of things that leave giant holes for the writer to fill in to get from one step to the next. There's a lot of explaining what things are and how they work, but they don't tell the reader how to create those things for themselves. In fact, it's a lot of analysis. Don't get me wrong. They're very educational, but being able to explain and understand the material makes you a potential critic who understands screenwriting and how it works, but it doesn't necessarily make anyone a writer. They're simply a more informed reader. This is a great thing, but it won't get someone who wants to write to the goal of writing his or her own screenplay.

PREWRITING YOUR SCREENPLAY is actually a true-to-form, step-by-step process by which you construct an original story (starting with absolutely nothing at all) through answering questions and completing exercises at the end of every single chapter until you have a complete and original story idea with the characters perfectly designed to serve that cohesive story. It's an instruction manual for putting together a story with all the elements that should fit perfectly together like a giant jigsaw puzzle. Then, the book ends by explaining how to do the whole process in reverse in case you're in a situation of having to fill in the blanks of a preexisting story idea.

The process explains to writers how I create a well-formulated foundation for a movie, whether working from a blank page forward or having to reverse engineer a soul into a preconceived plot idea. I give all I know and can think of to share with you. I'm keeping no secrets because there's never a reason to keep the logic of how things work secret. No two writers would execute the same idea the same way, so, even if you have my technique, you'd never execute it the way I would. It's everything that I learned and use when developing a project that has kept me writing as a decade-long, current and active WGA member.

I thought it was very interesting that you use the word "prewriting" in the book's title, as opposed to simply "writing".

What's the reasoning behind that, and how does prewriting apply to the craft of screenwriting?

Put simply, Prewriting is the opposite of rewriting. Rewriting is the work a writer does on a script after the first draft, and Prewriting is everything the writer creates before he or she writes the first draft. This entire book focuses on everything a writer needs to consider before writing "FADE IN," the old-school first words of a screenplay.

There are a ton of books that explain writing and formatting the actual script. Nobody needs to write another book that explains script format. It's been done to death.

This book explains how to assemble everything a writer needs in order to write a screenplay. It's the foundation a writer builds upon. There are many things a writer should figure out before leaping into an outline. Doing this work up front will save writers an enormous amount of time normally spent rewriting after the fact trying to make the story congeal. If time is money, this book can save writers a fortune in rewrites.

And because this book is strictly about how to develop a story concept with an incredibly strong foundation and structure, it is applicable to all mediums of storytelling. It's a universal storytellers playbook for formulating a cohesive narrative. I'm a screenwriter, so the examples throughout the book focus on films, but the logic of my foundation development for storytelling applies to any and all creative writing mediums, including stage plays, episodic series, comic books, novels, video games, animation, and all other media. In fact, someone told me they're going to start using my method to redesign history lessons to teach history to their students. It's applicable to anyone who can use storytelling in whatever they do to be more effective.

No doubt a lot of aspiring writers will use your book to improve their skills. Is there a particular piece of advice you think every writer should know?

Uh… My brain just exploded. That's a book in itself. It's a series of books! That said, I offer you these 10 pieces of advice:

If you think you can live happily doing anything else except screenwriting, this business is so obscenely tough, do something else. With books, you can self-publish. With playwriting, the production is not allowed to change the work without the playwright's permission. Even in television, there are far more opportunities, and the writers have more say. In film, the writers are hired guns and the director is the creative king. In television, the director is the hired gun, and it's the writers who develop the show and its seasons. I intend to make that jump when the timing is right, too.

Write what you love and would pay to see, not what's trendy.

Rejection is common, and you should never take it personally. When you're starting out, people are hesitant to bet on someone lacking experience. You need 50 to 100 rejections in order to get 1 yes. Even if you are not a good writer yet, you may find someone newer to the industry. This person may get what you're trying to do and wants to work with you.

Never argue about feedback with anyone giving you feedback as a friend or to help. You can ask questions for clarity, but once you understand the notes, thank the note giver profusely and shut the fuck up. Never argue. If you disagree with the notes, you simply don't apply them. They're bound to give you one or two notes that lead to a good change. Even a broken clock is right twice a day.

99% of the time the note giver is correct that there is a problem where they said a problem occurs in your script. 99% of the time, the solution they offer is incorrect. The difference between the note-giver and you is that you are the writer of this story. You will need to figure out how the problem needs to be fixed in order to best serve the story you want told.

Even a horrific writing experience or partnership is a good experience if you learn something meaningful from it.

When you agree to work with someone, get the full terms of your understanding in writing, even a co-writer.

Get in shape. I hate to admit it, but the entertainment business is a ridiculously shallow industry. People hire people they would want to spend time with, of course, and people want to spend time with those who look good and have the confidence that looking good provides them. You do not have to be attractive; you just need to be the best version of you.

You cannot be afraid to say no and walk away from a deal or offer. If the material isn't getting you fired up, or the offer is going to leave you feeling un-collaborative, it's best not to engage in something you don't feel really good about because that will leave an impression. You'll just end up not delivering and burning bridges, and there are only so many bridges in Hollywood because it's such a small industry. Saying no to things you do not feel engaged by is actually a very good business decision. I recently had a dear friend bring me a project with big name people involved. I read the script and instantly knew it wasn't for me. Friends and industry professionals understand and respect someone that isn't desperate. They smell desperation from a mile away and find it repulsive.

Always be working on multiple projects at a time. That one actually comes from Robert Zemeckis. I like to work on three. Producers have a slate of projects because they never know which one is going to get momentum or when it will happen. So should you. You never, as an artist, want to put all your eggs in one basket. That leaves the writer feeling desperate, and you know how Hollywood feels about people who are desperate.

You're listed as serving on the WGA's Writer's Education Committee. What is that, and what sort of things do they do?

There are several committees on which WGA members may serve. Some focus on diversity groups and others on general membership. One of the latter is the Writers Education Committee. It was created in 2002 to develop programs that provide WGA members with practical, insider knowledge about how the industry works and how it is changing, emphasizing tips and tools to help writers succeed. The goal is providing the most up-to-date working knowledge for writers.

I've chaired and served on a ton of panels for the WEC about the most current trends on going from spec script to studio green light, packaging, multi-platform storytelling, getting writing work with overseas producers, pitching in Hollywood, etc. Any WGA member can join the WEC, run ideas for educational events by the committee, assemble a sub-committee (if approved), and create the event of his or her own design.

You've also done a lot of lecturing and moderated panels about screenwriting. Are there any particular points or lessons you make sure to include as part of those?

Be true to you. The only thing no other writer in the world can do is be you. Figuring out who you are, what you stand for, and the original things you want to say to the world before you die will make you a one-of-a-kind writer in this or any industry.

Readers of this blog are more than familiar with my love/appreciation of pie. What's your favorite kind?

This is like asking that genre question again or asking someone to pick a favorite child. It's just not right. I love rhubarb, coconut cream, apple, pumpkin, banana cream, mixed berry (any berry really – blackberry, boysenberry… is cherry a berry?), and don't forget the oddly reptilian-named Turtle and Grasshopper pies. So long as it's filled with something tasty, how can you go wrong? It's pie. As long as it's not from Mrs. Lovett's Pie Shop in London, I'm game.

I would like to add one more thing. The shocking and most wonderful thing for me so far has been the reception my book has received when requesting consideration for an endorsement. You can see a bunch of their responses on the Amazon page under EDITORIAL REVIEWS, including the creators and/or show runners of such shows as LOST, THE BIG BANG THEORY, HAWAII FIVE-0, THE ORVILLE, screenwriters of THE DARK KNIGHT trilogy, STAR TREK reboot, BEAUTY AND THE BEAST, GUARDIANS OF THE GALAXY, icons like Stan Lee, and the most recent president of the WGA. After that are the endorsements from educators at AFI, USC, UCLA, NYU, and many more. You can read what they are saying and pre-order my book at: https://amzn.to/2HOMVFg.

Richard Walter

Originally posted: July 23 2021

Richard Walter is a novelist and author of best-selling fiction and nonfiction, celebrated storytelling educator, screenwriter, script consultant, lecturer and recently retired Professor and Associate and Interim Dean of the UCLA School of Theater, Film and Television where, for more than forty years, he chaired the graduate program in screenwriting. He has written scripts for the major studios and television networks, including the earliest drafts of AMERICAN GRAFFITI; lectured on screenwriting and storytelling and conducted master classes throughout North America as well as London, Paris, Jerusalem, Madrid, Rio de Janeiro, Mexico City, Beijing, Shanghai, Sydney and Hong Kong.

He is also a pop culture commentator, blogger and media pundit who has made numerous appearances on The Today Show, The O'Reilly Factor, Hardball with Chris Matthews, ABC Primetime, Scarborough Country and CBS News Nightwatch, among many other high-profile national television programs. More than a hundred newspaper and magazine articles have been published about him and the program he directed at UCLA.

What was the last thing you read or watched you considered exceptionally well-written?

The new bio MIKE NICHOLLS, A LIFE by Mark Harris.

How'd you get your start in the industry, and was that connected to you instructing at UCLA?

I came to California over fifty years ago for, I thought, three weeks, but fell into USC film school at the last minute, and never looked back. It was through faculty and classmates there that I learned screenwriting and made the earliest connections that led to professional assignments.

A little more than ten years later, at a glitzy showbiz party in Malibu, I was invited to join the faculty at UCLA. I was busy adapting my first book, the novel BARRY AND THE PERSUASIONS, for Warner Brothers, who had bought the film rights and hired me to write the screenplay. I was not seeking work. Still, as I would advise my children, you don't have to eat the whole thing, but at least taste it. I tasted teaching and found that it was the perfect complement to writing.

As someone who actually teaches screenwriting, is recognizing good writing something you think can be taught or learned?

Yes and no. No one needs education to decide what scripts or movies they like. That said, there's good evidence that studying the art and craft in a worthy program goes a long way toward launching and maintaining a career.

What do you consider the components of a good script?

First of all, story; that is, what the characters do and say. What they do and say also establishes who they are. Regarding the latter, that is, what the characters say, dialogue needs to be worth listening to all for itself, but it can't be all for itself. It needs at the same time also to advance the story and advance the audience's appreciation of the characters. Conflict, controversy, and confrontation are required throughout the narrative, and those are just the 'cons.'

What are some of the most common screenwriting mistakes you see?

Overwriting. Too many pages. Too much dialogue. Too much description, especially regarding instructions to the actors regarding pauses and gestures and such.

What story tropes are you just tired of seeing?

I'm weary of superheroes and comic-book adaptations.

What are some key rules/guidelines every writer should know?

Less is more.

Successful writing is not about adding paraphernalia to a narrative but taking it away, revealing a story that's somehow already there.

Don't have one character tell another what you've already told the audience.

Movies must appear real, but in fact they are fake. Writers should be wary, therefore, of writing 'the way it really happened' and creating dialogue that captures the way people 'really speak.'

What 'really happens' in life is, for the most part, boring. The way people 'really speak' is available in the streets for free, you don't need to go to the movies for that. Also, and again, the way people 'really speak' is, for the most part, tedious. Know what I mean? Get what I'm saying? Understand my point?

Have you ever read a script where you thought "This writer really gets it"? If so, what were the reasons why?

Sure. The give-away is economy: few words that reveal a lot, instead of the other way around. Nothing is present for its own sake but exclusively for the advancement of the narrative. Fancy language that might be appropriate in literature will swamp a screenplay.

**AUTHOR'S NOTE - I've often said one of the best pieces of writing advice I ever heard was "Write as if ink costs $1000 an ounce". Richard said that at a seminar of his I attended very early in my career. It really stuck with me, and I've used that as a guideline in my writing ever since.

How do you feel about screenwriting contests? Worth it or not?

There are some that are absolutely worthy.

How can people find out more about you and the services you provide?

Visit richardwalter.com. There's info regarding my books, limited-enrollment online screenwriting webinars, whose enrollees' scripts I'm willing to read, script consultation services, and more.

Readers of this blog are more than familiar with my love/appreciation of pie. What's your favorite kind?

Pecan. And I don't mind a scoop of vanilla ice cream on it.

David Wappel

Originally posted: Nov 27 2020

David Wappel is a screenwriter and story consultant. He recently wrote the screenplay for LONG GONE BY, now available on HBO Max, Amazon, and iTunes. Wappel worked in production and post-production for five years before turning to writing. His stories often feature themes of private courage, nostalgic longings, and contradictions.

He has consulted writers, producers, game developers, and others on their narrative work. In addition to screenwriting, you'll find Wappel talking about Tolkien, Shakespeare, or sailing.

What's the last thing you read/watched you considered to be exceptionally well-written?

This is a tough one for me, because I watch or listen to at least one Shakespeare production a week, and it's hard not to just answer with one of his plays.

So setting the Bard aside, the last thing I watched that was exceptionally well-written was an episode of STAR TREK: DEEP SPACE NINE titled THE VISITOR. Written by Michael Taylor, it's the second episode of season four of the series, and it's deftly simple and incredibly human.

I also recently rewatched DEAD AGAIN, written by Scott Frank. I've already seen it a handful of times, but I wanted to share it with my parents. What I love most about the script is the way it continues to surprise throughout, with twists and turns both big and small. It's like a rabbit hole that just keeps going down.

Oh, and if I'm not setting Shakespeare aside, the answer is The Globe's 2015 production of THE MERCHANT OF VENICE.

How'd you get your start in the industry?

I actually first started out working in post-production in Atlanta. I was an editor for a small production company. Editing is just writing with an extremely limited vocabulary. As an editor, you can only storytell with what is provided, and it's actually pretty amazing how much power you have to manipulate the moments by organizing shots in various arrangements.

So when I made the pivot into writing, I had already been looking at story as sequential bits of information, and it helped me understand how to build a moment, a scene, a sequence, or a story, piece by piece.

Is recognizing good writing something you think can be taught or learned?

I'm going to be a bit cheeky and say it doesn't have to be taught or learned. We already know when something is good writing from our emotional reaction. Humans are designed to have stories act on us emotionally. So instead of looking at a text and deciding if it is good writing or not, all you actually need to do is read it and look at yourself. If you're responding to it, it's good writing.

What isn't as apparent, but can be taught and learned is why something is good writing. One can study the patterns and structures, micro and macro, that seem to crop up again and again as effective ways to produce emotions in the audience. Writing, I believe, is both an art and a craft, and has tools and techniques like any other craft. How to employ those tools and techniques can be taught. Why to employ those tools and techniques is a little bit trickier, because it's far more subjective. That's what makes it art.

What do you consider the components of a good script?

When I'm reading, I'm looking for a few things. One thing I find myself sensitive to is honesty. Are the characters acting in ways that feel truthful. And that doesn't mean it has to be grounded, but it has to be truthful to the established world.

I'm also looking for specificity. Whether it's a feature or an episode of television, I value a script that is doing a "deep dive" into a specific aspect of the human condition. That may sound like it needs to be profound, but it doesn't. It just needs to be specific. Mediocre scripts tend to be about a general idea, but the great ones take a very specific idea, and explore it fully.

On a technical level, I value clarity. Not only do I want to visually understand what is happening, but particularly for the screen, I want to have a good sense of how I'm seeing it. For me, that's the biggest thing that separates screenwriting from other forms of writing, even playwriting. It's the explicit visual component, and the limitation of the lens. I don't need every shot selected, but I want a sense of how this will unfold on a screen.

In my opinion, a major component of a good script is restraint. I'm looking for human behavior, and nothing else. I want to see what characters are saying and doing, and draw my own conclusions. When I read a screenplay that tries to tease out meaning in the action lines (or even in the dialogue sometimes) I find myself checking out. It feels a bit like someone grabbing a puzzle piece and fitting it into the slot for you. People don't do puzzles just because they like how it looks when it's complete, they enjoy the act of completing it.

What are some of the most common screenwriting mistakes you see?

I think the most common screenwriting mistake I see is more of an artistic mistake than a craft mistake, and it's basically not having a specific enough answer to the question, "What are you trying to say?"

Corollary to that question is this one: "Why do you want to say it?"

Those two answers can act as guideposts for a writer, and will help navigate story choices. Without some reflection on these, a technically proficient story will end up vague and dull.

What story tropes are you just tired of seeing?

Honestly, none of them. What I'm tired of seeing are tropes lazily explored. Tropes are simply common patterns that are emotionally effective. What often happens is that more than the underlying pattern gets repeated, and we get bored of seeing the same thing over and over again.

For me, the key to keeping tropes fresh is to understand why they are tropes in the first place. What is the pattern beneath it? There's clearly a satisfying story element there, and going in the opposite direction to avoid a trope may be going in the opposite direction of that satisfying story element. You want to understand how it's working so that you can approach it, then zig-zag away in a specific way. You'll get all the benefit of a story pattern, without it feeling stale.

All that said, I'm completely over the "wife killed, husband wants revenge" trope.

What are some key rules/guidelines every writer should know?

This is in no way meant to be comprehensive or authoritative, but these are some guidelines I try to go by when writing.

Writing is 90% thinking and feeling, and 10% typing.

Melodramatic writing is not fixed on the page it occurs. It is fixed in all the pages preceding it, and then on the page it occurs.

A character's voice and a character's worldview are two different things.

People are different versions of themselves depending on who else is in the room. Characters should be the same.

Adjectives and adverbs may point to opportunities for stronger nouns and verbs.

Always be reading.

Wardrobe, makeup, props, and production design all provide storytelling tools. Make sure you're using them.

Turn off the critic for your first draft. After that, question every word.

When approaching a problem, see if it can be solved first by removing lines, rather than adding lines.

Understanding how your characters interact with the world outside of the story of your script can provide insight for how they interact with the world within it.

Have you ever read a script where you thought "This writer gets it"? If so, what were the reasons why?

Plenty of times, and while I'm sure it's different for everybody, for me the answer is in showing simple, specific moments of humanity. When I feel like a writer lasers in on something small, and then continues to explore each facet of it through a sort of narrative microscope, then I feel like I'm in good hands.

How can people find out more about you and the services you provide?

You can check out my website, davidwappel.com, and while I have a page on there about my services, it's also about me as a writer. The best way is probably to connect with me on Twitter - @davidwappel.

Readers of this blog are more than familiar with my love/appreciation of pie. What's your favorite kind?

Apple, by a mile.

Anat Wenick/The Write Script

Originally posted: Apr 30 2021

Anat Golan-Wenick started her career in the entertainment business working as a production assistant and researcher in a team that produced series for a large educational channel, while also pursuing a bachelor's degree in Film/Television and English Literature. After graduation, Anat moved to Los Angeles to dip her hands into the screenwriting pool. Her screenplays have won or placed in contests like Sundance Table Read My Screenplay, StoryPros, Scriptapalooza and others, with one getting optioned by the producer of THE LAST WORD with Shirley MacLaine and Amanda Seyfried.

After taking a script analysis class, Anat discovered her true passion in the entertainment business: reading and improving other writers' scripts. She became a reader for companies like Amazon Studios, Crispy Twig Productions, The Radmin Company, the Atlanta Film Festival and others, while developing connections with creative voices she aspires to bring to the big and small screens. In her spare time, Anat volunteers as the Secretary on the Board of the San Fernando Valley Writers' Club (a chapter of the California Writers' Club).

What's the last thing you read/watched you considered to be exceptionally well-written?

Not really "the last thing", but KIDDING on Showtime is a great example of how dialogue, visuals and story come together perfectly. Also on Showtime is I'M DYING UP HERE, which very skillfully weaves many plotlines together. Netflix's SHTISEL is an example of how a story about a seemingly insignificant part of the world's population can be made relatable. And for those catering to the younger audience, I recommend studying BOY MEETS WORLD. In terms of reading, THE CARTOONIST'S MASK by Ranan Lurie is a book I'd love to see adapted to screen.

How'd you get your start in the industry?

I always thought I would be a screenwriter. But an internship (followed by a full time position) at a TV station, working on a youth drama, set me on another course. I was a rookie intern when I was allowed to join my first script meeting. I sat quietly, just hoping to learn as much as possible, when the director, an amazing woman by the name of Yael Graf, turned to me and asked for my opinion. Without thinking, I said the solution won't work. A second later, I was mourning the loss of the best (and only) internship I ever had, when much to my surprise, the director actually wanted to know why I reached such a conclusion. Based on my explanation, the script was revised.

A few years later, I took a script reading class. Based on my analysis, the instructor encouraged me to pursue this career. My hope is to move from script reading to creative executive so I can work with undiscovered writers to help bring their stories to the screen.

Is recognizing good writing something you think can be taught or learned?

Akiva Goldsman once said: "Writing is both a pleasure and a struggle. There are times when it's really aversive and unpleasant, and there are times when it's wonderful and fun and magical, but that's not the point. Writing is my job. I'm not a believer of waiting for the muse. You don't put yourself in the mood to go to your nine-to-five job, you just go. I start in the morning and write all day. Successful writers don't wait for the muse to fill themselves unless they're geniuses. I'm not a genius. I'm smart, I have some talent, and I have a lot of stubbornness. I persevere. I was by no means the best writer in my class in college. I'm just the one still writing."

You can absolutely become a better writer. But just like any other job – if you want to be good at it, you have to study it, stay on top of new trends, and practice, practice, practice.

What do you consider the components of a good script?

Visual over telling. Don't say "he walks into a room," say "he skips, dashes, stumbles, falls, dances, shuffles into a room," etc.

Know the genre you're writing. Nothing wrong with a horror rom-com, but make sure characteristics of all genres are present in the script.

A well-executed "wait for it" moment. Scripts that constantly challenge me to wonder what will come next, even in based-on-true-event movies. Sure, we all know the Titanic is going to sink, but we wonder what will happen to the protagonists.

If you spend time developing your characters' external and internal conflicts, make sure to address them during the climactic moment. In CASABLANCA, Rick must get Ilsa and Victor safely to the airplane (external), while saying goodbye and convincing the love of his life to exit his (internal).

Good balance between dialogue and action sequences. Allowing the two to play off of one another, rather than feeding viewer/reader with a spoon.

What are some of the most common screenwriting mistakes you see?

- Excessive usage of voiceover for no reason. Personally, I'm not one of those "never voiceover" believers, but use it with caution.
- Unimaginative character description (i.e. JANE DOE, 26, pretty).
- Unnecessary camera and other directorial instructions as well as endless parentheticals in dialogue sequences.
- Undeveloped subplots.
- Usage of "Starts to," "Begins to," "Commences to," etc. as well as "beat." These phrases can kill the flow of a screenplay, especially when writing an action-adventure movie. Instead of using "beat", state what causes it (i.e. biting lip, looking away, cracking knuckles, etc.). Instead of "starts to walk but rethinks it," consider "marches off. Halts."

What story tropes are you just tired of seeing?

I would read anything, but if you're going to write about vampires or zombies, make sure you put a fresh spin or angle on the genre. WARM BODIES and INTERVIEW WITH THE VAMPIRE are two good examples. If writing a romcom, love doesn't have to be the ultimate goal. In WORKING GIRL, the protagonist wanted a career, and along the way she found love.

What are some key rules/guidelines every writer should know?

Read, watch, internalize, and execute in your own writing, repeat.

Connect with other professionals. You never know when an early connection will lead to a later opportunity.

When receiving comments, always thank the person even if you don't agree with them.

Your work may get rejected not because it's not great, but because it's not what the company is looking for. Do your research before sending.

Entertainment attorneys are a lot more approachable than agents and managers, and often can get your screenplay to the right hands.

People will have a more favorable view of you if when boasting about your achievements, you take a moment to acknowledge others. So when posting "my screenplay just advanced to quarterfinals/semi-finals/finals in "this and this" contest, add "congrats to all others who advanced" or "thank you for this opportunity", etc.

Even if making the slightest change to your script, make sure to save it as a new version. You never know when you may want to refer to an older version.

Always email yourself the latest version of your script, not just in PDF format, but in the writing-program-of-your-choice format, so you can restore the file if the software fails to open.

Ever in a slump and can't come up with an idea? Public domain is your friend. Either adapt a project, or use it as the base for your own interpretation (e.g. how EASY A was inspired by THE SCARLET LETTER).

Have you ever read a script where you thought "This writer really gets it"? If so, what were the reasons why?

The number of scripts I recommended can be counted on one hand. However, I have yet to encounter a project that was not salvageable, even those I scored extremely low. I encourage all writers to watch TOY STORY 3: Mistakes Made, Lessons Learned to realize we all struggle to "really get it."

How do you feel about screenwriting contests? Worth it or not?

Winning a contest can do wonders to boost the spirit, but winning alone will do nothing to advance a writing career, unless you build on the momentum. I recommend listening to Craig James, Founder of International Screenwriters' Association (ISA) advice on Screenplay Contest Strategy.

How can people find out more about you and the services you provide?

I mostly read for agencies, studios and contests. Screenwriters often don't want to hear the truth about their screenplays, they just want someone to say they're great, as Josh Olson wrote in his article "I Will Not Read Your F*%!ing Script". However, I have done quite a few free readings for aspiring screenwriters.

They can also find me through my website The Write Script (www.thewritescript.com), social media like LinkedIn and Twitter (@scriptslove), or through the San Fernando Valley Writers' Club, where I volunteer as a Board Member. Writers don't have to pay big bucks for a quality reading. Join a writing group or a writing community like Talentville that tells it like it is, and swap screenplays.

Do your research if you plan to pay for someone to read your script, especially if they boast about recommending your material to their contacts within the industry. I once encountered a person advertising his reading services on known screenwriting platforms, stating he was a final-round reader/judge for the Austin Film Festival and an Emmy Award Winner. Since the prices he charged were low for someone with such experience, I researched his claims and found out they were far from true. This is not to say the person didn't give good feedback, but writers can receive the same type of professionalism for much less, or even for free.

Readers of this blog are more than familiar with my love/appreciation of pie. What's your favorite kind?

I have yet to find a pie I haven't liked, and not for lack of trying. I volunteer as a tribute to boldly go where no pie lover has gone before to try new flavors. Has hazelnut chocolate cheesecake pie been invented?

(Author's note: it has.)

About the Author

Paul Zeidman is an award-winning screenwriter based in San Francisco who loves to create a ripping yarn that grabs the viewer and takes them on a rollercoaster ride of thrills and excitement that they can't wait to experience again.

He's also a notoriously meticulous script editor and proofreader, with the ability to spot a rogue comma or misspelled word at a hundred paces (give or take 99 paces).

When not writing, rewriting, or reading scripts, Paul enjoys watching movies, reading books in multiple genres, running somewhat long distances, and trying new recipes in the kitchen, along with making what could possibly be the best pecan pie west of the Mississippi.

Check out his screenwriting blog Maximum Z at http://maximumz.blog or follow him on Twitter: @maximum_z.

Made in the USA
Monee, IL
30 July 2022

10398245R00128